BRITISH RAILW

PAST and PRESENT

No 26

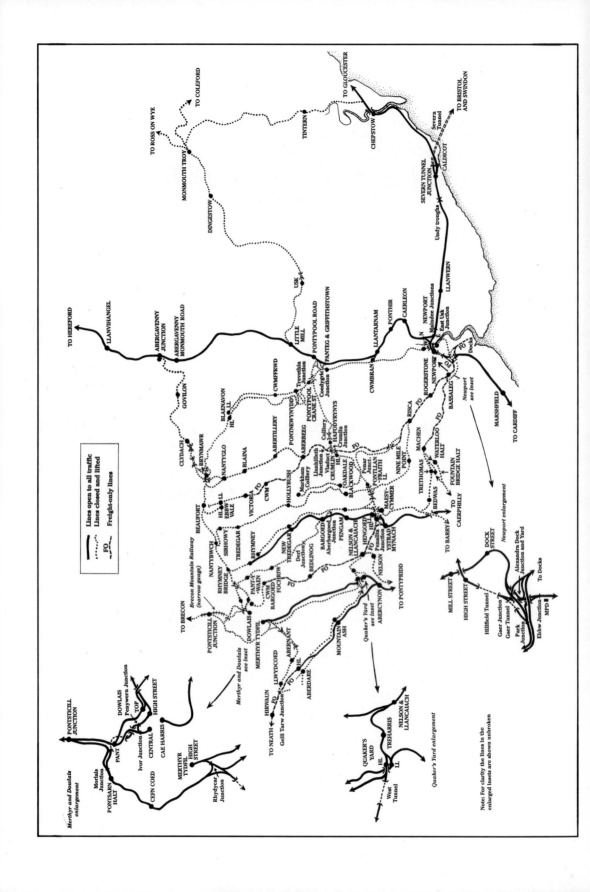

BRITISH RAILWAYS

PAST and PRESENT

No 26

South Wales
Part 1: Gwent and routes to Dowlais and Merthyr

Don Gatehouse & Geoff Dowling

Past and Present

Past & Present Publishing Ltd

This book is dedicated to the memory of
Jean Dowling (26 November 1941-27 August 1994)
and
Alan Gatehouse (17 July 1942-10 May 1994)

© Don Gatehouse & Geoff Dowling 1995

All rights reserved. No part of this publication may be reproduced, stored in a retrieval system or transmitted, in any form or by any means, electronic, mechanical, photo-copying, recording or otherwise, without prior permission in writing from Past & Present Publishing Ltd.

First published in November 1995

British Library Cataloguing in Publication Data

A catalogue record for this book is available from the British Library

ISBN 1 85895 082 1

Past & Present Publishing Ltd
Unit 5
Home Farm Close
Church Street
Wadenhoe
Peterborough PE8 5TE
Tel/fax (01832) 720440

Printed and bound in Great Britain

Maps drawn by Christina Siviter

CONTENTS

BIBLIOGRAPHY

History of the Great Western Railway, Volumes 1 & 2 *by E. T. McDermott and C. R. Clinker (Ian Allan)*
Forgotten Railways - South Wales *by James Page (David & Charles)*
Rails in the Valleys *by James Page (David & Charles)*
Railways of the Sirhowy Valley *by W. W. Tasker (Oakwood Press)*

Brecon & Merthyr Railway *by D. S. Barrie (Oakwood Press)*
Great Western Engine Sheds, 1947 *by E. Lyons (OPC)*
Great Western Coaches, 1890-1954 *by Michael Harris (David & Charles)*
Coal Society *by D. Egan (Gomer Press)*

INTRODUCTION

The development of railways in South Wales was not solely associated with the quest for better communication with Southern Ireland and the opening of the main line to West Wales. To a much greater extent the railway revolution was linked with the industrial growth that took place in the hinterland. Indeed, a large proportion of the railways of South East Wales were initially constructed as a successor to the canals and horse-worked tramroads as the method of transport used by the ironmasters of North Monmouthshire and North Glamorgan.

We therefore commence our brief review of the area's railways high above Merthyr Tydfil in the windswept and desolate land around Dowlais. It was here in the latter years of the 18th century that the local combination of iron ore, coal and limestone, together with fast-flowing streams fuelled by an abundance of rain, saw the development of the blast furnace and the production of pig iron.

The iron industry was to spread quickly eastwards along the Heads of the Valleys, to centres of production that included Ebbw Vale and Blaenavon. Initially, transport to the coast for shipment was made using pack horses and mules. Then the canals and tramroads were built to cater for the ever-increasing volumes of iron that had by 1839 made the Dowlais Iron Company the largest producer not only in Britain, but also in the world. With the development of steam traction, the increasing demand for coal, not only to fuel this new source of power but also to provide coke for the production of cast iron, was to herald the era of an industrial revolution that was to shape the social development of South East Wales for generations.

With coal being mined in ever-increasing quantities, the canals were also used to transport excess production to Newport for export. The potential for the development of rail transport was therefore immense and the second half of the 19th century was to see the construction of one of Britain's most intricate and intensively used systems. As a measure of the scale of railway building that was to cover South East Wales, the remote townships of Merthyr and Dowlais were ultimately served by six railway companies.

By the beginning of the 20th century the coal industry was well established with tens of thousands of men employed both in its excavation and in its transport by railways to markets within Britain as well as to the foreign ports of the world via the docks and wharves of Newport. The production of steel had superseded that of iron and, with local iron ore supplies long since exhausted, the need to import iron ore had seen the introduction of loaded mineral trains slogging up the valleys to the remaining centres of production at Ebbw Vale and Dowlais.

NEWPORT: Viewed from the end of the island platform at Newport station on 4 March 1961, ex-GWR Collett '7200' Class 2-8-2T 'Heavy Freight Tank' No 7252 takes the up through line with a loaded mineral train. The economic depression of the 1930s and the marked decline in coal traffic saw a number of the earlier '4200' Class 2-8-0T version of this locomotive type made surplus to requirements. To improve their operating range, the rear frames were extended and an enlarged bunker and trailing radial truck added. The locomotive illustrated was rebuilt in 1939 from the earlier Churchward locomotive No 4210.

March 1976 saw the introduction of the then heaviest train to run daily on British Railways, with the commencement of iron ore train workings between Port Talbot Docks and the BSC plant at Llanwern. Originally these trains, with a trailing load of over 3,000 tonnes, were hauled by three Class 37 locomotives, then in the mid-1980s pairs of Class 56 then pairs of refurbished Class 37 locomotives were used. More recently the Class 60 Type 5 machines have been allocated to the trains and No 60063 *James Murray* provides an appropriate contrast to our 1961 picture with a train of iron ore on the final leg of its journey to Llanwern on 12 April 1995. Note that the locomotive carries the Transrail branding, the new identity of Trainload Freight West that was launched in July 1994. *R. O. Tuck/GPD*

Within the overall infrastructure of South East Wales, Newport has always been a strategic centre for railway activity, both past and present. Situated at the intersection of the South Wales Main Line and the route to the North and Midlands via Hereford, it was also the focal point for railways built to serve the needs of the industrial hinterland.

At the Grouping of 1923, South East Wales had a density of railways unequalled anywhere within the national network. However, the South Wales coalfield had passed its peak year of production in 1913, when output exceeded 56 million tons, being 20 per cent of the overall UK production. The inter-war years were to turn South Wales into an area of mass unemployment, with the coal industry continuing its decline. The Heads of the Valleys mining communities suffered worst of all and a significant statistic recorded unemployment in Dowlais at 73 per cent in 1932.

Following nationalisation of the coal industry in 1947, the National Coal Board managed over two dozen collieries and employed over 20,000 men in the coalfields of Monmouthshire. However, re-organisation commenced in the early '50s in an effort to make pits more profitable and a succession of colliery closures was seen throughout the next four decades culminating in the end of deep mining in Gwent with the closure of both Marine and Oakdale collieries in 1989.

With the nationalisation of the railways in 1948, South East Wales was soon to suffer several closures, early casualties being the rural lines to Monmouth in the east and the Heads of the Valleys route across from Abergavenny Junction to Dowlais. The prosperity of the mining communities and that of its railways continued to decline with the contraction of the coal industry throughout the 1950s. The early '60s produced a spate of passenger service withdrawals, with certain routes only surviving until, in due course, their collieries ceased production and the last of the mineral traffic was lost.

Of the surviving system, much has been accomplished to upgrade rolling-stock in recent years. InterCity services are now operated exclusively by High Speed Trains and the Regional Railways services use modern 'Express Sprinter' units. Freight traffic volumes are still significant with the bulk of the activity associated with the British Steel plants at Llanwern near Newport and at Ebbw Vale. Open-cast coal is still mined in the area to the east of Merthyr and transported by rail from the disposal point at Cwmbargoed.

In presenting our portfolio of material covering Gwent and routes to Dowlais and Merthyr, we will provide you with an insight both into railways past and, where they are still active, a review of the present railway scene. Our work is not intended to be a complete history of the area as there are more detailed publications to be read on this subject.

Naturally, with such a large proportion of the former railway routes long since closed, the associated land has been re-developed or left to return to nature. Some may consider it futile to illustrate a present non-railway scene alongside a fondly remembered view of a bygone era, but there are now new generations of enthusiasts who would not otherwise know that there was once a railway where houses or industrial parks now stand, or along routes now followed by footpaths or roads.

We propose to take you on a series of journeys along the various routes that not only once served the communities within the valleys but also crossed the region from east to west. If this book manages to rekindle a few fond memories or educate others as to the extent of the railway system that once served this fascinating area, then we will have achieved our objective.

We offer our sincere thanks to the photographers who have allowed us to make use of their material and to the management and staff of the various subsidiary companies of British Rail for their assistance. Particular thanks are recorded for Alan Jarvis, Bob Tuck and John Hodge, who have also helped generously with information and advice on caption details. Finally, special thanks to Sue Gatehouse, who has supported us throughout this project with good humour and great cooking.

Don Gatehouse
Geoff Dowling

Chepstow and the Wye Valley

CHEPSTOW (1): I. K. Brunel designed and supervised the construction of the Wye Bridge at Chepstow during 1851/2. The bridge had an overall length of 600 feet, with half over the mud flats on the Monmouthshire side and 300 feet over the deep water to the cliff bank on the Gloucestershire side of the river, where the railway entered a deep cutting. The structure withstood the traffic demands of 90 years until, in 1944, part of the Monmouthshire span bent slightly under the stress of heavy wartime freight movements. For a number of years a 25 mph and later a 15 mph speed restriction was imposed over the bridge. In 1948 the Monmouthshire spans were re-girdered and in 1962 the remaining section of the Brunel structure was replaced. On 30 August 1960 Ex-'WD' 2-8-0 '8F' No 90448 approaches Chepstow with a down freight having just crossed the Brunel bridge and entered Monmouthshire.

The corresponding view taken on 9 April 1995 shows 'Express' unit No 158 794 working the 1155 Nottingham to Cardiff Central Regional Railways service. *R. O. Tuck/GPD*

CHEPSTOW (2): Chepstow station was situated at the eastern extremity of the South Wales Railway, the 75-mile section to Swansea having opened on 18 June 1850. Following the opening of the Wye Bridge in 1852, the link between the South Wales and the Gloucester and Forest of Dean Railways was completed. Freight sidings were provided on the down side of the line, with the goods shed on the up side, at the west end of the station. On a dull 3 January 1959 '5700' Class 0-6-0PT No 3726 arrives with the 1340 service from Newport.

Our view of Sunday 9 April 1995 shows unit No 158 833 approaching with the 1605 Cardiff Central to Birmingham New Street. The sidings on the down side are still in situ but unused, and the former goods shed has been incorporated into the premises of a builders' supply merchant. *R. J. Buckley/GPD*

11

TINTERN: The Wye Valley Railway introduced passenger and goods services between Chepstow and Monmouth (Troy) on 1 November 1876. The line was worked by the GWR from completion and the mainstay of the motive power on passenger services during the steam era was provided by the auto-fitted Pannier and '1400' Class locomotives, with diesel railcars being introduced by British Railways. On 15 September 1949, ex-GWR railcar W23W stands at the island platform at Tintern while working the 11.50 Monmouth Troy to Chepstow. Tintern was the only crossing place on the picturesque Wye Valley line, with other locations on the route being in the main served by unstaffed halts, although several did have adjoining goods facilities.

Following closure of the line, Tintern station site was purchased by Gwent County Council and the station building and signal box renovated. The site is now incorporated into the Wye Valley Walk and provides a museum and picnic area for visitors, as illustrated in our view of the site on a delightful spring day in April 1995. *R. J. Buckley/GPD*

MONMOUTH TROY was the focus of all passenger services that linked Ross, Pontypool, Chepstow and Coleford. In addition, the adjacent goods yard was for a number of years served by three daily workings, one from each of the three through branches. Indeed, in the 1950s on a typical midday, Troy station could be a hive of activity with three passenger and two freight trains on view. In a more tranquil scene taken on 9 May 1958, push-and-pull-fitted '6400' Class No 6431 takes water prior to working the 6.20 pm to Chepstow. Between the auto-trailer and the station building the portal of the 148-yard-long tunnel can be seen. The tunnel was of twin bore although one of the lines through was only a siding, the other being the line to Usk.

January 1959 saw the end of passenger services at Monmouth and the goods services were withdrawn in November 1964. Local agricultural and coal merchants occupied the goods shed and yard following closure and the station buildings provided accommodation for a local haulage contractor. However, all of the station buildings had been demolished by the time of our visit of April 1994 and only the brickwork of the former platform ramp in the foreground and the arch of the tunnel portal provided a visible physical link between the two views. *R. O. Tuck/DCG*

The South Wales Main Line to Newport

SEVERN TUNNEL: In an effort to improve rail access to South Wales, Charles Richardson proposed a tunnel linking Pilning to the South Wales Railway at Rogiet. Work commenced on the tunnel under the Severn estuary in 1873 and it was opened to traffic in 1886. The Severn Tunnel is 7,666 yards in length and at the peak of construction over 3,600 men were employed on the works. On the approach to the western portal, a deep cutting nearly 300 yards in length was excavated and this provided base material for the expanse of sidings to be laid adjacent to the new station near Rogiet, later named Severn Tunnel Junction. On 25 August 1960 ex-GWR 4-6-0 'Castle' Class No 5003 *Lulworth Castle* approaches the tunnel's western portal with the 10.29 Manchester to Penzance service. The train comprises an assortment of coach designs from pre-nationalisation companies as well as British Railways standard stock.

The corresponding view of April 1995 shows the 0932 Swansea to London Paddington InterCity Great Western HST service providing a marked contrast in both motive power and coaching stock design of the modern railway. *A. F. Smith, Peter Rowe (Printers)/GPD*

SEVERN TUNNEL JUNCTION MPD: Opened in 1907, the original shed was a standard Churchward straight road depot, having four roads under twin bays. In 1939 an extra bay was added and the coaling stage was extended. By the early 1940s a standard repair shop had been constructed at the rear of the shed, and at nationalisation it had an allocation of over 90 locomotives. The view taken on 12 October 1959 shows, from the left, locomotives Nos 4164, in lined green, 3846, 6903 and 3834. Note the absence of the circular vent in the brick gable end of the later constructed extension bay.

Closure of the shed was effected in October 1965 and the shed buildings and offices were subsequently demolished, with the site being used for motor vehicle storage for a number of years. Only the derelict structures on the site of the former repair shop survived at the time of our 1994 visit. *Hugh Ballantyne/DCG*

SEVERN TUNNEL JUNCTION (I): From pre-Grouping days there had been sorting sidings at Severn Tunnel Junction. Construction schemes during the 1930s, the early 1950s and then in 1960/2 saw the expansion of the freight handling facilities to provide 'hump' yards on both the up and down sides. This view looking westwards from the station in August 1961 shows ex-GWR 'County' Class 4-6-0 No 1013 *County of Dorset* on an up passenger working taking the Tunnel route. The down yard is on the left of the main line and the up or Undy yard is in the distance beyond the Middle signal box.

During the next 25 years, freight movements centred on the yards was considerable. However, following a review of Railfreight activities in South Wales, the decision was taken to concentrate all Speedlink freight activity at Gloucester and the yards at Severn Tunnel Junction were closed in November 1987. The recovery of infrastructure soon followed and our August 1994 view of a Swansea to London Paddington HST provides clear evidence of the clearance of this once thriving centre of freight activity. *A. F. Smith, Peter Rowe (Printers)/DCG*

SEVERN TUNNEL JUNCTION (2) provided platforms on both the Tunnel and Chepstow roads. Passenger services calling at the station have over the decades of British Railways operation been in the main secondary or local services operating between Cardiff and either Gloucester or Bristol Temple Meads. Our view of the station taken on 2 June 1957 shows ex-GWR '2800' Class 2-8-0 No 2874 on a down iron ore working from Banbury and clearly illustrates the extent of the facilities once provided for passengers.

Rationalisation has taken its toll in the intervening years, as evidenced by the corresponding view taken in August 1994, with 'Express' unit No 158 830 passing with the 0924 Portsmouth Harbour to Cardiff Central Regional Railways service. *John Hodge/DCG*

UNDY YARD: As part of the modernisation of the Severn Tunnel Junction Yard in 1960, ten reception sidings were provided for the up or Undy Yard. These additional sidings are visible to the left of the main line behind ex-GWR '2800' Class 2-8-0 No 2861 passing on the Down Relief road with a train of empty mineral wagons on 14 May 1960. Following closure of the up hump yard in 1981, these reception roads were used by Speedlink freight services for about two years prior to the concentration of such traffic into the main yards to the east.

On Friday 14 April 1995 a Class 158 'Express' unit passes with the 0824 Portsmouth Harbour to Cardiff Central service. The infrastructure that was visible in the 1960 illustration was removed during May 1988 and only the expanse of the former trackbed provides an indication of the extent of the freight facilities that were once provided. *John Hodge/DCG*

UNDY TROUGHS on 14 May 1960 play host to an ex-GWR 'Castle' Class locomotive on an up passenger train replenishing its tender. Note the water tank structure between the down lines, and the entrance to Undy Yard behind the locomotive. 'Castle' Class locomotives were the mainstay of South Wales express passenger services until the introduction of diesel-hydraulic traction in the 1960s.

In our August 1994 illustration power car No 43103 heads the 0715 Swansea to York Inter City service at the same location. Re-alignment of the Down Relief line, housing developments at Undy village and the progress of nature illustrate the passage of time. *John Hodge/DCG*

UNDY HALT: A timber halt was provided to serve the local community at Undy from 11 September 1933 until its closure on 2 November 1964. Access to the main-line platforms was via a footbridge that spanned the four tracks, and it is this structure that provides a link between our two illustrations. On 30 July 1960 BR Class '9F' 2-10-0 No 92248 passes on a Summer Saturday working from Cardiff.

A more elevated view taken in August 1994 shows Class 47/0 No 47292 rounding the curve with 4E68, the 0720 Pengam FLT to Lynmouth Alcan RfD Freightliner (Contracts) empties. The locomotive had worked from the North East overnight and had earlier delivered a trainload of aluminium ingots to the Cardiff Freightliner terminal. *R. O. Tuck/DCG*

NEWPORT EAST SIGNAL BOX: Immediately after crossing the River Usk viaduct, down trains would enter Newport station. The view taken on 4 March 1963 shows ex-GWR 'Castle' Class No 4078 *Pembroke Castle* arriving with the 11.55 London Paddington to Swansea service. On the left is Newport East signal box, which was opened on 29 May 1927 to house a power-operated interlocking frame used for controlling the semaphore signalling. The limited space available between the running lines and the houses to the rear of the signal box forced the engineer to adopt a pedestal arrangement for the structure, with steel brackets under the front of the cabin to support the overbalanced position.

The box controlled the former Maindee West Junction and Newport East for 34 years until superseded by the 'panel' box commissioned in December 1962. On 29 April 1994 Class 47/4 No 47582 *County of Norfolk* takes the Down Relief line with the 1037 Bristol Temple Meads to Swansea empty NPCCS working. *R. O. Tuck/GPD*

NEWPORT (HIGH STREET) (1) was first opened on 18 June 1850 by the South Wales Railway. During 1875-78 the station was enlarged, and following the Grouping the GWR completed further construction work in 1928. On 30 August 1961 ex-GWR 'Castle' Class 4-6-0 No 7021 *Haverfordwest Castle* sets off for Cardiff with the 3.55 London Paddington to Fishguard Harbour service. The journey of 261¼ miles from London to West Wales would take just under seven hours in total. Visible in the background above the first coach of the train is the earlier 1878 building, behind which is the 1928 five-storey down-side office building. On the right of the loco-motive is the extensive Newport Goods Depot.

In the early 1960s a major re-organisation at the station took place, following which passenger traffic was concentrated on the island platform. Comparison of the two pictures confirms that the former platform 5 was re-numbered to be platform 2, with down passenger services now using this platform. On 12 April 1995 Class 60 No 60036 *Sgurr Na Ciche* returns empty tanks to West Wales from Heathfield in Devon. The 19th-century office structure has been demolished and the land formerly occupied by the Goods Depot, closed in August 1972, has been used for road improvements and car parking for rail passengers. *Hugh Ballantyne/GPD*

NEWPORT (HIGH STREET) (2): Major track alterations and colour light re-signalling was completed in the early 1960s in anticipation of the increased freight traffic associated with the newly opened Llanwern Steelworks. The through roads at Newport station have carried a regular flow of freight activity for decades and this brace of illustrations provide a contrast in both rolling-stock and motive power for their respective eras. On 12 July 1952 '5100' Class 2-6-2T No 5155 provides a flurry of exhaust at the head of a mixed train comprising both timber and steel mineral wagons.

The April 1994 view shows Class 60 No 60062 *Samuel Johnson* hauling loaded PTA iron ore tipplers *en route* from Port Talbot Docks to BSC Llanwern. The first Class 60 locomotives were allocated to the Trainload Metals freight sector in South Wales in 1990, for crew familiarisation prior to their introduction into regular revenue-earning service the following year. The sight of these up-to-date Type 5 workhorses at the head of these heavy trains typifies the trainload bulk haulage capacity of the modern railway. *John Hodge/GPD*

NEWPORT (HIGH STREET) (3): With the completion of the reconstruction work in 1878, High Street station was enlarged to enable all of the Newport Valleys services to be concentrated at the one location and provide passengers with a direct interchange with main-line services. Trains to and from the valleys would use the platforms to the north of the station site through into the British Railways era. On 12 July 1952 ex-GWR railcar No W21W stands at platform 7 awaiting departure on its next turn of duty on an Eastern Valleys working. Between 1922 and 1941 C. B. Collett was the Chief Mechanical Engineer of the GWR and one aspect of railway development in which he led the way was in the use of diesel railcars. One of the second batch of 15 such vehicles, No 21 was built at Swindon in 1941. This second batch of vehicles had a more angular appearance than earlier-built versions and were equipped with buffers and standard drawgear to enable them to haul a tail load of up to 60 tons.

The withdrawal of the remaining passenger services in the Newport Valleys and the re-organisation of the station layout and associated train operations in the early 1960s saw platform 6 re-numbered to be platform 3 and since that time to be served by up passenger train workings. Our view of the former platform 7 in April 1994 shows it still in situ, but unused. 'Dutch'-liveried Class 37/0 No 37207 has just completed its rostered duties for the morning and is approaching the Godfrey Road Stabling Point accessed from the west end of the platform road. *R. C. Riley/GPD*

NEWPORT, GODFREY ROAD CARRIAGE SIDINGS occupied land on the north side of the station site and for many years provided storage and servicing facilities for the various rakes of steam-hauled coaching stock used principally on the Newport Valleys services. Our August 1961 view shows '5700' Class Pannier tank locomotive No 3671, which was rostered to perform station pilot duties, standing at the entrance to the fan of carriage sidings.

With the demise of steam and the spate of withdrawals of local passenger services in the early 1960s, activity at Godfrey Road Sidings was considerably reduced, and eventually the number of sidings needed for operation requirements was rationalised. Our corresponding view of April 1994 confirms that much of the site is now given over to car parking. The remaining sidings are used to store engineering stock that includes the adapted wagons used for work in the Severn Tunnel. With Newport High Street now a train crew depot, diesel locomotives are also stabled at Godfrey Road Sidings between their duties based on activity at the nearby Alexandra

Dock Junction and East Usk Junction Yards. A point of architectural detail to note when comparing the two illustrations concerns the Newport Civic Centre buildings visible in the background; the clock tower was added to the main structure in the early 1960s. *David Mathew/DCG*

The Eastern Valleys

CWMBRAN JUNCTION: The Monmouthshire Railway & Canal Company (MRCC) opened its line from Newport to Pontypool via Cwmbran on 1 July 1852. When the GWR opened its route from Pontypool to Newport via Caerleon, a connection between this line at Llantarnam and the MRCC line at Cwmbran was opened in 1878 and the original station at Cwmbran was replaced by GWR passenger facilities sited on the new spur. With the diversion of all Eastern Valleys passenger services via the new route and into Newport High Street with effect from March 1880, the former MRCC line south from Cwmbran to Mill Street was henceforth only used by goods and mineral traffic for Newport Docks until through running on this route ceased in 1963. In the view taken on 7 May 1960 an RCTS/SLS special negotiates the junction at Cwmbran. The scene is viewed from across the Monmouthshire & Brecon Canal, originally built in 1792 to carry coal and iron ore traffic and in turn made redundant by the MRCC railway. Beyond the leading auto-trailer can be seen the GWR station and the line to Llantarnam Junction.

The May 1994 view confirms that no trace of either the railway or canal can be seen and only the distant buildings provide suitable points of reference. *S. C. L. Phillips/GPD*

PANTEG & GRIFFITHSTOWN (1): In 1854 the Newport, Abergavenny & Hereford Railway made a connection with the MRCC at Coedygric Junction to the south of Pontypool, and to cater for the increased traffic to and from Newport the MRCC line was doubled. The station that served Panteg & Griffithstown was sited immediately south of the Coedygric Junction and had staggered platforms with the goods yard sited opposite the down platform. On 24 May 1956 '5600' Class 0-6-2T No 6675 of Pontypool Road shed (86G) was rostered for an Eastern Valleys additional service for Barry Island. Viewed from beneath the canopy of the main building on the up platform, the locomotive is seen waiting to take the empty stock up to Blaenavon Low Level.

Although closure of the line to passenger traffic came in 1962, the station building has survived and is used by a local building contractor; our view taken in April 1994 shows that even the canopy is still in situ. *R. J. Buckley/GPD*

PANTEG & GRIFFITHSTOWN (2): Viewed from the south end of the up platform, railcar W4W arrives with the 7.45 Newport to Pontypool Road service on 24 May 1956. Behind the down platform the steelworks of Richard Thomas & Baldwin Limited provide the industrial skyline. The prototype of these streamlined diesel railcars was built by AEC Ltd of Slough and first introduced in December 1933. Vehicle No 4 was one of the small batch built and introduced into service in July 1934. These later cars had two 121 bhp engines, one to each bogie, and were capable of speeds of over 75 mph. They were intended for express services, had seating for 44 passengers and were fitted out with a small buffet. Initially they were used on a high-speed service between Birmingham and Cardiff, with the 117-mile journey being covered in 139 minutes, including three stops. They were not designed to work in multiple or with a trailing vehicle, although there was a concealed drawgear and simple buffers for use only in an emergency. At the time of nationalisation in January 1948 only the former GWR routes operated regular diesel railcar services in Britain. With the introduction of the new diesel multiple units in the late 1950s withdrawals of the 35 surviving railcars commenced, and by the end of 1962, all had been displaced. Fortunately, examples have been preserved and vehicle No 4 is now part of the National Collection.

In our corresponding view in April 1994 the steelworks still provide the industrial backdrop, but the population of chimneys has been somewhat reduced. The goods shed is also still in situ, being used by a local coal merchant; the building is just visible behind the bushes to the right of the path that now follows the former track alignment at this location. *R. J. Buckley/DCG*

PONTYPOOL, CRANE STREET (1) was the first station in the town and the terminus for the MRCC services to and from Newport when the line opened on 1 July 1852. The MRCC had originally built an engine shed for the branch locomotive, but this facility lasted only until 1878, when the shed closed. On 24 June 1956 the 8.50 service from Newport High Street arrives behind '5700' Class 0-6-0PT No 9667. On the left passengers, having purchased their tickets, take a seat in the sun to wait for the next southbound service to Newport.

The station closed from 30 April 1962, when the Eastern Valleys passenger services were withdrawn. However, the original 1852 MRCC buildings were not demolished until November 1991, when in a careful operation the bricks and stones were removed to the Pontypool & Blaenavon Railway's Furnace Sidings site for future re-construction. The land at Pontypool was cleared and used as part of a road development, which now enables through traffic to avoid the town centre. The view taken in April 1995 illustrates the total transformation of the former station site. *R. J. Buckley/DCG*

PONTYPOOL, CRANE STREET (2): During 1853 the MRCC line was extended north from Pontypool through Pontnewynydd and some two years later the southern end of the route saw Newport Mill Street connected to Dock Street, the then terminus for the Western Valleys traffic. By 1870 the mineral branches to the north-west of Pontnewynydd had been opened and with these various connections completed between the industrial areas and the docks, the railways of the Eastern Valleys enjoyed significant prosperity. During this period the extent of the competition posed by the neighbouring GWR had culminated in the MRCC entering a leasing arrangement in 1875, which in turn produced complete amalgamation in 1880. By the early 1900s the demands for new motive power to cater for the developing mineral traffic of South Wales had lead the GWR to introduce the '4200' Class 2-8-0T. These Churchward mineral tank engines were specifically designed for the short haul from pithead to port or power station, and the prototype was introduced in 1910. Our September 1936 view looking north from the station footbridge at Crane Street illustrates a typical down mineral train with a '4200' Class locomotive working bunker first.

A car park now occupies the site and the gable end of the Globe Hotel building provides a point of reference with our April 1994 view of the location.
W. Potter/GPD

PONTYPOOL, CRANE STREET GOODS: The small goods yard at Crane Street was sited on the down side and accessed by trains from the north end of the station. Our second view taken in September 1936 shows a GWR Pannier tank shunting wagons in the busy yard. A feature of mineral and goods workings in the valleys was the 'target' number displayed on a white disc carried by the locomotive, target E13 seen here being an Eastern Valleys working.

The goods yard closed from 31 October 1966, although the line remained open for goods and latterly coal traffic until eventual closure in 1980. The iron railings and lamps of the pre-war railway era have long since passed into history, with no visible trace of the site's former use in our view taken of the car park in April 1994. *W. Potter/DCG*

34

TREVETHIN JUNCTION: As early as 1948 British Railways had commenced an examination of future motive power requirements. In due course the review identified the need to develop the diesel railcar for fleet use, especially for branch lines and local services, many of which were still operated using coaching stock dating back to pre-Grouping days and hauled by equally venerable steam locomotives. In 1957 British Railways introduced its Derby three-car diesel multiple units (DMUs), and by the following year members of the South Wales allocation had been put into service on Eastern Valleys passenger duties. Alas, the introduction of modern diesel trains could not save the flagging fortunes of the local services that plied the Newport Valleys, and the withdrawal of passenger services came in 1962. On 23 April, a week prior to the end of passenger services, a DMU threads its way along the valley side near Trevethin Junction as it heads north from Pontypool Crane Street for Blaenavon Low Level.

As elsewhere in the vicinity of Pontypool, many of the former railway lines have been used to develop new roads for the traffic demands of the 1990s, and our view of the site in April 1994 shows the location totally changed. The spread of housing developments in the intervening years is also clearly evident. *Michael Mensing/DCG*

BLAENAVON LOW LEVEL (1): Following the conversion to a railway of the former tramroad that had been constructed in 1796 to serve the coal and iron industries of the Blaenavon area, the MRCC commenced goods traffic north of Pontnewynydd from 1 June 1854 and began to run passenger trains to the new terminus at Blaenavon from October of that year. The lower section of the line was subsequently doubled, but the portion just north of Cwmffrwd to Blaenavon remained single track and was worked by electric train token. To distinguish it from the former LNWR/LMS station, BR added the suffix 'Low Level' to the former GWR station in 1950. On Sunday 29 April 1962, the final day of services on the line, a three-car DMU waits to leave with the 7.30 working to Newport.

Following closure of the line, the tracks were lifted and the land eventually used for a housing development, with blocks of flats now occupying the site. *Hugh Ballantyne/DCG*

BLAENAVON LOW LEVEL (2): The tracks continued for a short distance beyond the north end of Blaenavon Low Level station and in the days of steam the sidings were used to stable the locomotive and stock prior to its being propelled back to the down platform. On 21 August 1957 auto-fitted '6400' Class 0-6-0PT No 6429 simmers in the afternoon sun prior to working back down the valley to Pontypool. The train comprises an all-3rd coach next to the locomotive and an auto-trailer, No W161W, of 1929 vintage; the latter was built during the GWR's bow-ended era of coach design, and was one of the first of three batches of such saloons built for general branch-line service between 1929 and 1933. Design features of note were the 7-foot pattern bogies and the small inward-opening hammered glass ventilators set above the compartment windows.

As with the station site nearby, the land was used for a housing development following closure of the line, leaving little trace of the former railway. When pin-pointing the corresponding view in 1995 the church tower provided a suitable reference point, and even several of the former railway fence-posts could still be seen amongst the trees that have now grown in the foreground. *Ian L. Wright/DCG*

BLAENAVON (HIGH LEVEL): Blaenavon was the original terminus of the LNWR branch from Brynmawr and opened to passengers on 1 January 1870. The buildings and adjoining goods shed were of stone construction and by 1899 a brick-built engine shed had been provided. The locomotive allocation was outstationed from Abergavenny and was for use on local coal traffic. LNWR 'Coal Tanks' were originally allocated, but in the mid-1920s they were displaced by the large 0-8-4 tank engines that had been introduced by the LMS for such work in the South Wales valleys. The Depression of the '30s saw much of the local traffic lost and passenger services were withdrawn from 5 May 1941. Henceforth Blaenavon was served by the former MRCC station lower down in the valley and closer to the town centre. The shed was closed from 5 September 1942. British Railways added the suffix 'High Level' in 1950, by which time only freight traffic used the line. In our view of the station taken on a dull 20 July 1957, No 5231 waits for the road with a train of empty mineral wagons bound for Furnace Sidings. The goods yard was eventually closed from 28 September 1964.

When visited in May 1994 only the remains of the former down platform provided any confirmation that the station and associated facilities were once sited here, all trace of the former buildings having gone. *Rev R. W. A. Jones/DCG*

38

FURNACE SIDINGS, BLAENAVON: To the north of Blaenavon were the collieries and ironworks that were the source of considerable freight traffic over many decades. The line beyond Furnace Sidings to Brynmawr was closed from 24 June 1954, but the line to Llantarnam Junction continued to generate freight traffic until the Big Pit Colliery ceased production on 2 February 1980 and closure of the line was effected in June of that year. Our final view of Blaenavon shows an unidentified Class 37 flogging up the final stretch of its climb to Furnace Sidings with a train of empty MDV wagons for re-loading with coal. The 309-strong fleet of English Electric Type 3 diesels was introduced between 1960-65 and a sizeable allocation was received in South Wales. They soon established themselves as the staple motive power on a wide range of freight activity, none more significant than the movement of coal down the valleys.

In the April 1994 view the scene has changed little. The track has been left in situ after closure as the Big Pit Colliery site and the remains of the Blaenavon ironworks were developed into a working museum. Also the Pontypool & Blaenavon Railway preservation Group has established their base on the site of the former Furnace Sidings. *R. L. Masterman/DCG*

Newport to Llanvihangel

CAERLEON (1): We now turn our attention to the line from Newport as far as Llanvihangel on the route to Hereford. Approaching Caerleon from the south on 2 June 1957, ex-GWR 'Grange' Class 4-6-0 No 6823 *Oakley Grange* and 'Modified Hall' '6959' Class 4-6-0 No 6969 *Wraysbury Hall* pass Caerleon signal box at the head of the 2.05 Bristol Temple Meads to Manchester Piccadilly. For over two decades following nationalisation, through services between the West Country and the North West of England and the Midlands would use this 'North and West' route, prior to changes that saw these workings re-routed via Gloucester and the former Midland line using the Lickey Incline.

Just as the 'Grange' and 'Hall' Class locomotives were the maids of all work in the steam era, the Class 37 has been arguably the most successful and widely used of the 1955 Modernisation Plan designs. The refurbishment programme of the mid-1980s saw selected locomotives receive complete internal rebuilds, and the 37/4 sub-class comprised 31 variants fitted with electric train heating (eth) equipment and allocated to Scotland and South Wales for passenger duties. Despite the introduction of 'Sprinter' units on the majority of passenger ser-

vices along the Welsh Marches route, the Class 37/4s have maintained an ongoing presence. Our May 1994 illustration sees one of the former Scottish-based locomotives, No 37407 *Loch Long*, passing with the Sunday 1315 Cardiff Central to Liverpool Lime Street service. *John Hodge/DCG*

CAERLEON (2): Viewed from the road overbridge that overlooks the north end of the station, ex-GWR '6400' Class 0-6-0PT No 6429 propels a local service away from Caerleon on 21 July 1957. Diesel multiple units were introduced on the Eastern Valley services during the following year, but in due course these local services were withdrawn from 30 April 1962 and the station closed.

Our visit in May 1995 found the main station building surviving with part of the premises in use as a veterinary clinic. The remainder of the former station forecourt and goods yard area have been redeveloped as a trading estate. A Class 158 'Express Sprinter' unit passes with a Regional Railways service from Manchester Piccadilly to Swansea. *Rev R. W. A. Jones/DCG*

PONTHIR: The Pontypool, Caerleon & Newport Railway (PC&N) opened its line initially to goods traffic on 17 September 1874 and to passengers on 21 December of that year. Ponthir was one of several stations on the line opened at that time. Prior to the opening of this alternative route from Pontypool, GWR trains would run by way of Coedygric Junction to reach Newport at Mill Street station for passengers, and beyond via Dock Street for freight. However, the 8 miles and 73 chains from Pontypool Road South Junction to Maindee West Junction enabled the GWR to divert all of its traffic away from the Eastern Valleys section of the Monmouthshire Railway. On a sunny 20 June 1957 ex-GWR '5101' Class 2-6-2T No 5171 restarts its two-coach train away from the down platform on a Pontypool Crane Street to Newport working.

As at Caerleon, Ponthir had a stone-built station building sited on the down platform, but the latter structure had long since been confined to history by the time of the visit made in May 1994, when 'Dutch'-liveried Class 37/0 No 37197 was photographed passing the former station site *en route* to Newport. *John Hodge/D. E. Moon*

LLANTARNAM JUNCTION: The Great Western Railway opened the short connecting branch between Llantarnam Junction on the Caerleon line and Cwmbran Junction on the Monmouthshire Railway line (see page 28) in April 1878. With the provision of this link, all Eastern Valley passenger services into Newport Mill Street ceased in 1880, being diverted into the enlarged High Street station. The 1975 view of Llantarnam Junction shows a southbound freight hauled by an unidentified Class 47 passing the former GWR signal box that controlled the junction. By this time the link through to the Eastern Valleys was provided for freight-only traffic and following the closure of the Big Pit at Blaenavon the line beyond the Junction closed with effect from 8 June 1980.

On Sunday 1 May 1994 Class 153 unit No 153 373 passes the site with the 12.55 Hereford-Cardiff Central service. The rate of growth of the conifer trees that had been planted behind the signal box at the time of the 'past' picture is plain to see, with the tower block in nearby Cwmbran almost totally obscured from view. *R. L. Masterman/GPD*

PONTYPOOL ROAD (1): Viewed from the road overbridge to the south of the station, ex-GWR 4-6-0 'King' Class No 6023 *King Edward II* was photographed on 19 May 1962 departing with a southbound passenger service. This was in fact the last day of operation of the 'King' Class locomotives on the 'North and West' route south of Shrewsbury. The locomotive was taken out of service in the following month as part of the first batch of withdrawals, which saw the remainder of the Class condemned by the end of the year. Fortunately, No 6023 was subsequently rescued from the cutter's torch and purchased for preservation.

The extent of the rationalisation of the railway infrastructure can be seen when comparing the above scene with that of Friday 10 July 1992, in which a pair of Class 37/0 locomotives, Nos 37051 and 37138, pass with 6V78, the 1520 steel empties from Dee Marsh Junction to Margam. Part of the dual-carriageway Pontypool bypass road has replaced the former freight avoiding lines on the west side of the site, and only the main building on the down side of the station has survived the considerable rationalisation of this once important junction station. *R. O. Tuck/DCG*

45

PONTYPOOL ROAD (2): At the north end of the station a single-line bay platform was provided for services for Monmouth Troy, and on a wet 28 May 1953 ex-GWR railcar W30 awaits its next turn of duty. The passenger service to Monmouth in the early 1950s comprised four return trips on weekdays only, and approximately 45 minutes was allowed for the journey of 18 miles, with eight intermediate stations/halts being served. Note the collection of BR teacups at the base of the lamp post!

Some 40 years on and the concept of the single-car unit is still a feature of railway travel. The Leyland Class 155 two-car formations were originally introduced in 1987 for longer-distance provincial services. In August 1990 the first members of the Class were arriving at Hunslet Barclay Ltd in Kilmarnock to be converted and re-numbered as Class 153 single-car units, and in the spring of 1992 six of the initial batch released into service were allocated to Cardiff. With corridor connections at each end, these 23-metre-long units could revert to working in multiple or be added to other train formations to strengthen services at peak times. On Sunday 10 April 1994 Unit No 153 380 heads away from Pontypool Road with the 1150 Newport to Hereford service. *Alan Jarvis/GPD*

PONTYPOOL ROAD SHED and the adjoining marshalling yard, which comprised over 50 sidings, were developed at this key site location, being both alongside the main line that linked South Wales to the North West of England and the Midlands and also in close proximity to the junction with the line from Neath and the Eastern Valleys route. The brick-built roundhouse shed was opened in 1865 and some four years later the stone-built straight shed was added. To the north of the main locomotive shed buildings was sited the coaling stage illustrated in this September 1936 view. This large brick-built facility with a slated pitched roof was a 1898 replacement for the earlier coal stage, that was in fact retained for the water tank that formed the roof of the structure. The raft of wagons on the ramp comprises examples of the 20-ton iron loco coal and mineral wagons built by the GWR to improve the efficiency of the movement of Welsh coal. Much research had been undertaken from the turn of the century on the economics of larger-capacity wagons. With the annual production of Welsh coal in the region of 50 million tons, the use of 9-, 10- and 12-ton capacity wagons was clearly inefficient. A 20-ton wagon was chosen as it represented the largest-capacity mineral wagon that could usefully be carried on four wheels given the condition of many of the colliery sidings served.

The depot closed from 31 May 1965, and the site was eventually cleared. With the construction of the Pontypool by-pass road, a traffic island now occupies the former coaling stage site, but there is a petrol filling station close by to serve the fuelling needs of present-day motive power! *W. Potter/GPD*

LITTLE MILL: The Newport, Abergavenny & Hereford Railway Company was incorporated in 1846 and the line between Hereford, Barton and Coedygric Junction, Pontypool, where it continued via the Monmouthshire Railway's line to Newport, opened on 16 January 1854. The marshalling yard at Pontypool was the focal point for numerous freights that traversed the route and was the destination of this assortment of wagons behind ex-ROD 2-8-0 No 3038 pictured just south of Little Mill Junction on 28 July 1951. These heavy goods engines based on a Great Central Railway design were first ordered in 1917 to supply the needs of the Railway Operating Division of the Royal Engineers for the war effort in Europe. Following the end of hostilities, the Government disposed of their surplus engines and the GWR purchased and fully overhauled a number of them. Complete with Swindon superheaters, GWR-pattern safety valve, cab-side numberplates and re-numbered 3038, our subject locomotive was allocated to South Wales and worked in the area until withdrawal in July 1956.

The advance of lineside vegetation is all too evident in our view taken in May 1995. A Cardiff-bound Regional Railways service operated by 'Express' unit No 158 839 passes at speed. *R. O. Tuck/B. Cole*

USK: At Little Mill Junction we will take a brief detour along the Monmouth line, the first station encountered being Usk. The station was set on a narrow site against a wooded hill through which a 256-yard tunnel was cut to take the line on to Monmouth. To the west of the station the line crossed the river via a plate girder viaduct to where the goods yard was located. Passenger services between Monmouth and Pontypool Road ceased in May 1955, while goods services were withdrawn beyond Usk a month later and between Glascoed and Usk in September 1965. The line from Little Mill Junction to the Royal Ordnance Factory at Glascoed remained in use for freight traffic until the early 1990s. Our original view of Usk station was taken in 1955 just prior to closure, and the wholesale return to nature in the intervening years is all too apparent in the corresponding picture (*middle left*) taken in the spring of 1994. The footpath follows the former platform, but the density of growth totally obscures the masonry of the tunnel mouth, which is shown in the bottom view taken from the site of the demolished station building. *Rev R. W. A. Jones/GPD (2)*

DINGESTOW: The Coleford, Monmouth, Usk & Pontypool Railway (CMU&PR) completed its single line from Little Mill Junction on the Newport, Abergavenny & Hereford Railway to Monmouth (Troy) on 12 October 1857. The line was then extended to Wyesham and in due course to Coleford. The railway was built to carry iron ore as well as pit wood and farm produce to supply the industrial areas of the South Wales Valleys. Unfortunately, the anticipated volumes of Forest of Dean iron ore traffic over the completed CMU&PR did not reach fruition and the route assumed the status of a rural branch line almost from the outset. Dingestow was typical of a number of the stations on the line, with a single platform and cattle dock more than sufficient for the respective levels of traffic. On 12 October 1957, two years after closure, the last train to work between Monmouth Troy and Pontypool Road was a two-coach SLS special hauled by '5700' Class 0-6-0PT No 4668. The train, operated to mark the centenary of the line, paused at the weed-infested platform at Dingestow, where the retired station master turned out in his Edwardian Great Western Station Master's attire to greet it.

Our corresponding view of May 1994 shows that the former station building has survived in private ownership. Indeed, it has been given a new lease of life, with the canopy still visible, being incorporated into the timber extension of one of the farm buildings that now occupies the site.
Rev R. W. A. Jones/GPD

ABERGAVENNY JUNCTION station was opened by the LNWR to serve the needs of passengers to and from the Heads of the Valleys line, and the station sign on the down platform in our view taken on 23 August 1957 confirms the need to change for Brynmawr, Tredegar and Merthyr. A northbound freight trundles through in the charge of ex-GWR '4300' Class 2-6-0 No 5347. These mixed traffic 'Mogul' locomotives were first introduced in 1911 by G. J. Churchward, and the engine illustrated was one of the batch delivered from Swindon during the later years of the First World War, when demand for such versatile machines required a number to actually see service in France prior to their return to the GWR in 1919.

With effect from the introduction of the summer working timetable of 1958, the semi-fast passenger services

between Cardiff and Hereford went over to diesel multiple unit operation. With the introduction of the new services, the number of intermediate stops was reduced and saw the closure of the smaller stations along the route, including Abergavenny Junction, which closed from 9 June of that year. The corresponding view some 37 years later records the passing of 'Express' unit No 158 833 with a Cardiff-bound service. Note the small retaining wall still inset into the embankment. *John Dew/B. Cole*

52

ABERGAVENNY, MONMOUTH ROAD: We now return to the main line, and travel north to Abergavenny. Opened by the Newport, Abergavenny & Hereford Railway on 2 January 1854, this station received the suffix 'Monmouth Road' in 1950 to distinguish it from Abergavenny Junction. However, following the closure of the latter station, the suffix was dropped and British Railways reverted to the original name. During the steam era a banking engine was usually required for northbound freight trains, as the ruling gradient from the River Usk at Penpergwm through and beyond Abergavenny was 1 in 82, easing to 1 in 95 before the summit of the climb to Llanvihangel. On 24 August 1957 ex-LNWR 0-8-0 '7F' No 49403 slowly approaches the rear of a northbound freight to provide assistance. The locomotive would not be coupled to the brake van and upon reaching Llanvihangel would drop away from the rear of the train.

The goods yard on the right remained open until April 1981 and the goods shed survives and is in commercial use. On 13 May 1995 Class 37/0 No 37178 provides the contrasting light locomotive subject of our corresponding view from the station footbridge. The locomotive has just delivered a rake of empty spoil wagons to the sidings at the south end of the former goods yard in preparation for weekend engineering work and is about to return south to Newport. *Ian L. Wright/GPD*

LLANVIHANGEL station had a staggered platform arrangement and closed in June 1958. By the time of our photograph, some seven years later, the down platform had been removed completely and only rubble marked the remains of the former up platform, which can be seen to the right of the passing 4.50 Cardiff General to Hereford DMU service. These three-car Cross Country diesel mechanical units were introduced in 1958 and built to Derby specifications by the

Gloucester Railway Carriage & Wagon Company. The leading car of the formation illustrated was the Driving Motor Brake Composite (DMBS), the centre Trailer Buffet Second TBS(L) had a small buffet area with a counter at the one end, and the rear car was the Driving Motor Second, Lavatory DMS(L). Under the TOPS classifications the units became Class 119.

During the early 1980s the Cross Country DMUs were displaced by locomotive-hauled stock on the through services, and by the end of that decade modern 'Sprinter' units had arrived on the scene. The Class 158 'Express Sprinters' were introduced on South Wales Regional Railways passenger services in May 1991 and these two-car units now provide the standard train formation on the route. On 20 May 1995 unit No 158 833 is working the 0845 Cardiff Central to Manchester Piccadilly service. *Michael Mensing/GPD*

55

Heads of the Valleys

ABERGAVENNY JUNCTION: The Heads of the Valleys line was authorised in 1859 and made a junction with the Newport, Abergavenny & Hereford Railway near Abergavenny. Before the railway opened as far as Brynmawr on 29 September 1862, the London & North Western Railway (LNWR) had leased the line, and it was that company that provided the locomotives and rolling-stock for the commencement of operations. The LNWR opened its station about a mile north of the town centre of Abergavenny, providing a passenger interchange with the Newport to Hereford line. The station illustrated in this view taken on 23 August 1957 was the 1870 replacement for the original passenger facilities. Ex-GWR '5700' Class 0-6-0PT No 5728 awaits departure with a brace of ex-LMS coaches forming an evening passenger train for Merthyr.

Closure of the station was effected from 9 June 1958 and the site has subsequently been put to use by local industries, a number of whom had long since vacated their respective plots when our corresponding view was taken in 1994. *John Dew/GPD*

ABERGAVENNY MPD: Opened by the LNWR in November 1867, Brecon Road MPD was rebuilt to provide a 12-road shed some years later. The locomotive allocation included for many years a number of the LNWR 0-6-2T 'Coal Tanks'. Their short wheelbase together with a relatively high power output made them ideal for the sharp curves and stiff gradients in the area. Following nationalisation, control passed to the Western Region, but the depot still had a North Western flavour with over a dozen ex-LNWR 0-8-0 'G2s' allocated there. In this view taken on 14 September 1952 the roofing from part of the shed had been removed.

With the decline in freight traffic the shed was reduced to a stabling point in late 1954, and closure came in January 1958. The stone buildings were later demolished and modern industrial units were available to let when the site was re-visited in 1994. *W. Potter/DCG*

GOVILON: The Merthyr, Tredegar & Abergavenny Railway was promoted by a group of local ironmasters in order to upgrade the means of transport to serve the iron industry that had developed along the northern boundary of the South Wales coalfield. Upon leaving Abergavenny and crossing the River Usk, the line commenced a 9-mile climb that had a ruling gradient of 1 in 34. The first community west from Abergavenny to be served by the MT&A line was Govilon, where there was a small coal yard adjacent to the station. From September 1954 auto-fitted Pannier tanks from Merthyr shed worked the majority of passenger trains, and '6400' Class No 6427 is seen arriving with a westbound service from Abergavenny in August 1957.

The station building remains in situ and has been modified and extended to provide a private dwelling. Note also the former platform edge at the base of the garden fence on the right. In 1991 a Brecon Beacons National Park Project saw the construction of a section of the Newport to Abergavenny cycle path, which now follows the former trackbed between Abergavenny and Govilon. *Rev R. W. A. Jones/DCG*

CLYDACH: Upon leaving Govilon the train would have to tackle the 1 in 37 gradient to follow a tortuous route through the Clydach Gorge and then over open moorland towards Merthyr, which proved a considerable challenge to build and expensive to operate. High on the hillside overlooking Clydach Gorge the railway reached Clydach station, which was later downgraded to the status of a halt. The buildings, complete with fire buckets and the adjoining house, are well illustrated in this summer scene taken on 28 August 1957, with No 6423 on an auto-train for Abergavenny. Immediately beyond the west end of the platforms the line entered Clydach Tunnel, the separate bores of which were 302 and 330 yards in length.

The station survives in private ownership, complete with platforms and waiting shelters preserved in half of the site. However, the site is split between two owners, and the location required for our corresponding view of May 1994 had seen the advance of nature, although the upper windows of the station house can be seen through the trees. *Rev R. W. A. Jones/GPD*

BRYNMAWR had developed as a junction station with the opening of the branch to Blaenavon by the LNWR in 1869, and that to Nantyglo in 1905 by the Brynmawr & Western Valleys Railway. Both of these branch lines made end-on connections with the GWR, and prior to the Grouping the latter company had taken over the respective passenger services. On 3 May 1951 ex-LNWR 'G2' No 49403 awaits the right of way at the head of an Abergavenny-bound freight. Note the tender cab that was fitted on all locomotives of this Class allocated to work in the area. The station buildings were of timber construction, and a distinctive feature that provided a measure of protection against the elements was the enclosed footbridge.

The passenger services to Blaenavon had been withdrawn as early as 1941, those to Newport via the Western Valleys surviving until 30 April 1962. January 1958 saw the end of passenger services to Abergavenny and the station site at Brynmawr was soon cleared following the withdrawal of goods traffic in November 1963. No trace of the former station site is now visible. *R. C. Riley/GPD*

BEAUFORT: In 1864 the Heads of the Valleys route was extended west to Nantybwch, Beaufort being one of the two intermediate stations. Set in a cutting, the main station buildings were of stone construction with timber being used for the waiting shelter on the opposite platform. To the east of the station were sited the signal box and timber-built goods shed. On 21 August 1957 an auto-train calls *en route* to Abergavenny Junction. During the 1950s weekday services comprised five through workings each way between Abergavenny Junction and Merthyr Tydfil. Approximately 1 hour and 40 minutes was taken to cover the 24½-mile journey that had 15 intermediate stops. The station nameboards still read 'Change for Ebbw Vale', although passenger services, which actually ran from Brynmawr, had been withdrawn from the branch from 5 February 1951.

Following closure of the line, the station site was cleared and in due course the cutting in-filled to the level of the adjacent roads. The row of houses on the right of the picture taken in May 1994 provides the physical link between the two illustrations. *Ian L. Wright/DCG*

EBBW VALE (HIGH LEVEL): The single-track Ebbw Vale branch had been opened in September 1867 and in due course carried considerable freight traffic to and from the steelworks. The branch was less than 2 miles long and the station provided by the LNWR was of stone construction. A small goods yard with a single-road timber shed was sited opposite the platform. The 'High Level' suffix was added in 1950 to distinguish this station from the GWR's, which served the Western Valleys line. On 5 January 1958, nearly seven years after the withdrawal of passenger services, ex-LNWR stalwarts Nos 58926 and 49121 visited the branch with an SLS special. The track to the right of the locomotives continued south beyond the station to serve the steelworks. An industrial line ran behind the station platform and was used for carrying limestone from the quarries at Ystrad, near Trevil. The branch line eventually closed in November 1959 when coal traffic from Tredegar ceased.

Our view of the location in May 1994 confirms a total transformation, with a multi-storey car park now dominating the site. All Saints Catholic Church remains a prominent reference point to link the two illustrations. *R. J. Buckley/DCG*

NANTYBWCH (1): West of Brynmawr the MT&A line crossed open moorland that was nearly 1,200 feet above sea level. Passenger services as far as Nantybwch were introduced on 1 March 1864 and it was here some four years later that the Sirhowy Railway arrived from the south. On 14 August 1957 auto-fitted locomotive No 6423 arrives with the 3.15 Abergavenny Junction to Merthyr Tydfil service. The Sirhowy Valley lines are in the right foreground.

The scene on a sunny day in May 1994 shows young children enjoying the recreation facilities that now occupy this part of the former station site. It is clear that the houses in the background have been subject to a number of structural alterations and improvements in the intervening 37 years. *R. O. Tuck/DCG*

NANTYBWCH (2): Following its acquisition of the Sirhowy Railway in 1876, the LNWR had direct access to Newport and through services from Nantybwch were once a feature of the passenger timetable. However, in the final years of operation an auto-train service to and from Risca was the norm, and in this view taken on the last day of passenger services, 11 June 1960, '5700' Class 0-6-0PT No 3634 has arrived with the 3.36 working from Risca. Although ex-GWR motive power had taken over in the mid-1950s, the Crewe influence remained to the end with the LNWR Type 4 signal cabin and the wrought iron lattice footbridge both dating back to standard designs of the late 19th century. Indeed, the single-line section from Sirhowy to Nantybwch was still worked using the train staff and ticket system until closure.

In our May 1994 view there is no trace of the site's former use and beyond the wooden fencing the A465 trunk road has cut across the formation of the Sirhowy line. *Hugh Ballantyne/GPD*

RHYMNEY BRIDGE: The LNWR extended the Heads of the Valleys line westward from Nantybwch in a joint venture with the Rhymney Railway and opened the line to Rhymney in 1871, thus providing a through route to Cardiff. Two years later the line to Dowlais from Rhymney Bridge was opened as another step towards Merthyr. On 2 November 1957 No 6427 pauses at Rhymney Bridge propelling coach W4030W and driving trailer W166W, forming the 10.03 Merthyr Tydfil to Abergavenny Junction. The LNWR lattice footbridge carried additional screening, glazed upper panels and corrugated roofing as a reminder of the often bleak and inhospitable nature of the local climate.

Much of the former trackbed was obliterated by the building of the A465 Heads of the Valleys trunk road, and our photograph of May 1994 had to be taken from the middle of a traffic island. The trees in the left background provide the link between the 'past' and 'present' views. *Hugh Ballantyne/DCG*

DOWLAIS HIGH STREET: In its continuing quest to reach Merthyr Tydfil, the LNWR opened the line from Rhymney Bridge to Dowlais on 1 January 1873, and it was from here that it joined the Brecon & Merthyr Railway in June 1879. The Heads of the Valleys line arrived at Dowlais high above the north-east side of Merthyr. From its station at Dowlais High Street the line commenced its descent via Pentywern Junction to either continue to Ivor Junction, where it joined the Brecon & Merthyr line to Dowlais Central station or via a tunnel beneath the B&M line to Morlais Junction, from where it continued on the joint line to Merthyr. Dowlais High Street station was opened on 4 May 1885 and was an all-timber structure incorporating the various standard LNWR features. It is therefore fitting that our final illustration of the LNWR route includes representatives of the two classes that were the mainstay of Crewe-designed motive power over the decades. On the final day of operation, 5 January 1958, Webb 'Coal Tank' No 58926 and 'G2' No 49121 have arrived at High Street station with an SLS special, being the last train on the Heads of the Valleys route.

Our May 1994 view of the site shows the former station house on the left and the trackbed now grassed over in the foreground and occupied by a dormer residence in the centre background of the picture. *E. T. Gill/DCG*

The Taff Vale Extension

PONTYPOOL ROAD: The incorporation of the Newport, Abergavenny and Hereford (Taff Vale Extension) Railway in 1847 marked the formal commencement of the westward route from Pontypool to make a junction with the Taff Vale Railway at Quaker's Yard. At Pontypool Road the GWR re-built station of 1909 featured a large island platform between the up and down lines, connected to the main buildings via a subway (see pages 44-45). A bay was provided at each end of the island platform and it was from the bay at the southern end that the 'Taff Vale Extension' services would operate. On 23 April 1962 '5600' Class 0-6-2T No 6661 waits to depart with the 11.00 to Neath.

Following the rationalisation of services in the early 1960s, the extensive facilities at Pontypool Road became redundant and the island platform was subsequently cut back with the removal of the bay platforms and the demolition of the buildings and canopies. The extent of the cut-back is clearly illustrated in our view from April 1994 showing a Class 153 unit passing. On 19 May 1994 the station was officially re-named Pontypool & New Inn. The ceremony marked the completion of a refurbishment that included demolition of the former GWR station building to clear space for increased 'park and ride' facilities, re-surfacing of the platform, new signage and lighting and a new public address system linked to the signal box at Little Mill.
Michael Mensing/DCG

HAFODYRYNYS COLLIERY: Travelling through the narrow Glyn Valley to the west of Pontypool, the line reached the site of Hafodyrynys Colliery. Pictured amongst the colliery buildings on 8 May 1971 is an RCTS Eastern Valleys Rail Tour, which employed three-car Cross Country DMU set No BL510. At that time the colliery still had its own steam shed, visible on the left of the scene, and enthusiasts travelling on the rail tour were clearly enjoying the sight of hybrid Ebbw Vale/Peckett 0-4-0ST No 37, formerly named *Nasmyth*, in steam outside the shed.

Following closure of the line between Pontypool Road South Junction and Trosnant Junction in June 1964, the line from Trosnant Junction to Hafodyrynys Colliery remained open until 1979 to provide rail access to the colliery. The site was then cleared during the 1980s to allow a new road to be built along the former trackbed, and our view taken in May 1994 shows both the new road alignment and the former route of the A472 that passed to the north of the colliery site. *Hugh Ballantyne/DCG*

GLYN VALLEY: At the west end of Hafodyrynys Colliery was a miners' halt that was served by unadvertised trains from Pontypool Road until November 1961. Upon leaving the colliery complex, the line then curved sharply following the contour of the valley to descend towards a short tunnel to the south of Hafodyrynys village and enter the Ebbw Valley. On 14 October 1963 '5600' Class 0-6-2T No 5638 on a westbound freight from Pontypool Yard drifts down towards the eastern portal of the tunnel. These mixed-traffic tank engines were specifically designed and built to operate in the South Wales Valleys. The GWR had acquired many engines from the former Welsh railways at the Grouping that were in a deplorable condition and fit only for scrap. As a consequence, C. B. Collett decided to build a new standard design of 0-6-2T that was to prove a versatile and powerful workhorse for many decades. The first batch, which included No 5638, was built at Swindon in 1924-5.

Although closed for many years, the track alignment at this point was still easily recognisable when photographed in the spring of 1995. *W. Potter/DCG*

GLYN TUNNEL, HAFODYRYNYS: The original objective of constructing the Taff Vale Extension line was to provide a link to the areas around Merthyr and Dowlais and the wealth of potential traffic generated by the iron-works. However, with the start of the expansion of the coal-mining industry, it was this latter commodity which would provide the bulk of the freight activity that was to use this outlet to the English markets. Ultimately, a through route to Swansea was to be completed via the Vale of Neath in August 1864. During the years of construction the line had passed into the hands of the West Midland Railway in 1860, and in turn the GWR. Work on the 280-yard Glyn Tunnel at Hafodyrynys was commenced in the autumn of 1853 and was completed to enable the line from Pontypool Road to the east side of the valley at Crumlin to be opened on 20 August 1855.

Viewed from above the west portal of the tunnel on 14 October 1963, '5600' Class No 5601 flogs eastbound with a train of empty bolster wagons. In the distance can be seen Hafodyrynys platform.

Following closure of the line, the tunnel was in-filled and in due course the profile of the land altered when road widening was undertaken. Our corresponding view of 1995 shows a picnic area now occupying part of the site. *W. Potter/DCG*

HAFODYRYNYS PLATFORM was opened on 1 May 1913, being unstaffed from 1932, and was sited to the west of the village close to where the road passed under the railway. The railway at this point was set on a shelf on the hillside and the Neath-bound platform was of the customary timber construction to conserve weight. On 12 June 1964 '5700' Class 0-6-0PT No 3717 approaches with a westbound service from Pontypool Road. The west portal of Glyn Tunnel is visible in the background. In the 1961 timetable of passenger services there were eight through workings in each direction between Pontypool and Aberdare on weekdays only, five in each direction scheduled to call at Hafodyrynys Platform. The journey time for the 22¾ miles was approximately 1 hour 10 minutes, with 12 intermediate stops.

Little trace of the railway alignment remains at the location today, with the former embankment removed during a road widening scheme undertaken following the closure of the line. *W. Potter/DCG*

CRUMLIN JUNCTION, set on the east side of the Ebbw Vale, was linked to the Monmouthshire Railway Company's Western Valleys line below by a branch that was opened on 20 August 1855. This single-line connection from Llanhilleth Junction 1 mile 25 chains to the north never had a public passenger service, although it was used by workmen's trains until April 1961. Our view taken on 6 May 1962 shows '5600' Class 0-6-2T No 6656 on an SLS Special coming off the connecting line. Above the locomotive is the single track crossing Crumlin Viaduct. The line from Pontypool Road had been doubled soon after it had opened and, while the viaduct was constructed for double-track operation, the GWR carried out extensive work to the decking in the 1920s and single-track working over the viaduct remained the operational practice until closure.

The corresponding view taken in May 1994 shows the masonry abutments of the viaduct still in situ, now providing a viewing platform and a splendid vantage point high above the Ebbw Vale. *E. T. Gill/DCG*

CRUMLIN JUNCTION TO LLANHILLETH JUNCTION: On 27 June 1963 English Electric Type 3 (later Class 37) D6866 commences the descent to Llanhilleth Junction. The locomotive illustrated was numbered under the 1970s BR TOPS re-classification as 37116, and in the late 1980s it was rebuilt to become one of the Class 37/7 Railfreight Petroleum Sector variants, No 37891.

Closure of the line to goods traffic came on 17 May 1964, although the alignment is still easy to identify some 30 years later. *W. Potter/DCG*

CRUMLIN VIADUCT (1): At Crumlin, the Ebbw Valley is narrow and precipitous and the Taff Vale Extension line would be required to cross some 200 feet above the valley floor via a unique viaduct 1,650 feet long. The contractor, T. W. Kennard, commenced work on the viaduct in the autumn of 1853. His design comprised a structure of braced cast-iron tubes and girders that, unlike a masonry viaduct, would present a minimum cross-section to the wind and lessen the resultant force imposed on such a sizeable structure. The result was a masterpiece of engineering, being both practical and graceful. On 31 October 1962 the low autumn sun breaks through the passing clouds to highlight the viaduct structure as an ex-GWR 2-8-0 tank crosses with a westbound freight.

Only the top of the nearside masonry abutments and the rows of terraced houses on the far side of the valley provide a link between the two illustrations.
W. Potter/DCG

CRUMLIN VIADUCT (2): The viaduct was completed in May 1857 and following Board of Trade inspection was opened for traffic a month later, when the Taff Vale Extension route was completed as far as Tredegar Junction, being just over 10 rail miles from Pontypool Road. The viaduct was in fact built in two spans separated by an intermediate hill. The main span was 1,066 feet in length and the smaller west span 584 feet. The view from Crumlin High Level station on 12 June 1964 shows ex-GWR '5100' Class 2-6-2T No 4110 with a Pontypool to Neath train crossing the west span.

Originally scheduled for preservation, lack of post-closure maintenance saw the fabric of the viaduct deteriorate to the extent that it had to be dismantled in 1967. Only the masonry abutments high on the valley sides mark its course, as shown in our view taken in May 1994. *W. Potter/DCG*

CRUMLIN (HIGH LEVEL): Having crossed the viaduct, westbound trains would arrive at Crumlin High Level station. The station nameboards confirmed that passengers for the Western Valleys should change there. However, the Low Level station was approximately a quarter of mile away and nearly 200 feet lower down in the Ebbw Vale. On 28 March 1964 the crew of '9400' Class 0-6-0PT No 9488 are about to receive the single-line token from the signalman on duty at Crumlin High Level signal box to enable them to proceed across the single-line section to Crumlin Junction.

Following closure of the route in June 1964 the station site was cleared, apart from the station house, which is now the residence of the last Station Master of Crumlin High Level. *T. J. Edgington/DCG*

PONTLLANFRAITH (LOW LEVEL): Tredegar Junction, later to be re-named Pontllanfraith, was where the Taff Vale Extension crossed the Sirhowy Valley. On 4 April 1960 our photographer was the subject of attention for both the passenger and waiting railway staff rather than ex-GWR 0-6-2T No 5679 arriving with a Neath-bound train. In British Railways days the 'Low Level' suffix had been added to differentiate between this and the neighbouring 'High Level' station on the Sirhowy Valley line.

Following closure the station site was cleared to make way for a road development. Our May 1994 view was taken from the central reservation of the section of dual carriageway now occupying part of the former trackbed. St Augustine's Parish Church has had a single-storey church hall built on the ground formerly occupied by sidings and the church car park takes up the remainder of the site. The alignment of the trackbed leading to Crumlin is just visible to the left of the church hall. *E. T. Gill/DCG*

HENGOED (HIGH LEVEL): The line from Tredegar Junction (Pontllanfraith) through to Quaker's Yard was opened in January 1858. Upon leaving the Sirhowy Valley, the Taff Vale Extension passed through Maesycymmer Tunnel and entered the Rhymney Valley. At the west end of a masonry viaduct (see overleaf), Hengoed High Level station was reached. The end of the station platforms extended over the bridge that carried the line over the Rhymney Railway line and our view taken on 27 September 1958 shows the riveted girder section of the overbridge in the foreground. Ex-GWR 2-6-2T No 4593 has just arrived with the 7.40 service from Pontypool Road and has been given the right of way for its onward journey to Nelson & Llancaiach. The bracket signal also controls access to the spur that descends to the Rhymney Railway's line at North Junction, Ystrad Mynach.

With the closure of the line and the subsequent removal of the overbridge, the relative position of the Low Level station is revealed in our corresponding view of 1994; the end of the latter's down platform ramp can just be seen in the bottom left of the frame. *R. J. Buckley/DCG*

HENGOED JUNCTION: On 27 October 1962 '5100' Class 2-6-2T No 4169 has just crossed the Rhymney Valley with the 2.18 Pontypool to Neath train. The valley has been crossed via the graceful Hengoed Viaduct, a masonry structure of 15 arches, under which the former Brecon & Merthyr Railway line also passed on the east side of the valley. In the background of our 1962 view is also Hengoed Junction signal box, which controlled access to and from the former Rhymney Railway line, and Hengoed High Level station can be seen in the left distance.

Although largely hidden from sight in our corresponding view taken in 1994, Hengoed Viaduct has survived the closure of the railway it once carried and stands as an industrial monument. The former track alignment can be traced by the fence posts in the foreground. *John Dew/DCG*

NELSON & LLANCAIACH (1): When the Taff Vale Extension was opened throughout in 1858, the station at Llancaiach also served the nearby village of Nelson, until the provision of passenger services to Nelson from the south via the Taff Vale Railway's line from Pontypridd in 1900. With the opening of the Taff Bargoed branch to Dowlais in 1875 Llancaiach station was to prove inadequate for the increased levels of passenger activity, so in 1910 the GWR opened a substantial replacement station, Nelson & Llancaiach, complete with adjoining goods yard. On 4 April 1960 ex-GWR 0-6-2T No 5679 stands at the down platform with a Pontypool Road to Swansea service. On the far side of the island platform a connecting Dowlais service can be seen.

Following closure of the station in 1964, the buildings remained in situ until they were finally demolished in 1972. The view taken on Saturday 28 April 1990 shows Class 37/5 No 37697 passing with a local trip working comprising 14 loaded MDV wagons from Nelson East sidings. The coal loaded in the wagons had been stored at Nelson pending its return to Taff Merthyr Colliery's rapid loading bunker, for onward movement for power station consumption. *E. T. Gill/DCG*

NELSON & LLANCAIACH (2): On 28 March 1964 ex-GWR 2-6-2T No 4157 enters the up platform with the 11.05 Neath to Pontypool Road. On the left mineral wagons can be seen at the entrance to the adjoining goods yard. In the final years of operation, passenger receipts over the route had declined considerably and complete closure under the Beeching Plan was inevitable.

NELSON AND
LLANCAIACH

The section of the Taff Vale Extension between Penallta and Taff Bargoed Junctions has, however, remained in use for coal traffic. Until the closure of the collieries at nearby Taff Merthyr and Deep Navigation, there were regular movements of coal and colliery spoil trains through the former station site. However, it is the open-cast coal from Cwmbargoed that now provides the sole source of traffic on the route, and on Monday 25 March 1991 Class 37/7 Nos 37887 and 37797 draw their MGR train of loaded coal hoppers off the Taff Bargoed branch while *en route* to Aberthaw Power Station. *T. J. Edgington/DCG*

85

TREHARRIS: The final station on the route from Pontypool Road before the Taff Vale Railway was reached served the mining community of Treharris. Our view taken on 5 June 1964 from the rear of a Pontypool Road to Neath train hauled by an unidentified ex-GWR 2-6-2T '4100' Class shows a solitary passenger waiting on the bench outside the up platform shelter. The station booking office was set above the platforms at road level and can be seen above the roof of the platform shelter.

By the time of our visit to the location in 1994 the road bridge had been demolished and the station site converted into a recreation area. A garage now stands on the site once occupied by the booking office, and mounted on it is the salvaged and restored Treharris Pit hooter. The local colliery was known originally as Harris's Navigation Pits, after the principal shareholder, who also gave his name to the village that grew up around the colliery. For over a century the colliery produced the best quality Welsh steam coal until its closure in 1991.
W. Potter/DCG

QUAKER'S YARD (HIGH LEVEL) (1): The Taff Vale Extension made its final descent to join the Taff Vale's Cardiff to Merthyr Tydfil main line in 1858, just south of Quaker's Yard Junction (Quaker's Yard Low Level). This station provided the destination for trains from Pontypool until 1864, when the line from Aberdare was completed to Quaker's Yard East Junction and the adjacent High Level Station was opened on the new through route. Quaker's Yard village takes its name from the Society of Friends' burial ground situated there, but the station of that name was closer to the nearby village of Edwardsville. Viewed from the embankment beyond the down platform on the last day of services over the line, 13 June 1964, ex-GWR 4-6-0 No 6836 *Estervarney Grange* restarts the 2.25 Pontypool Road to Neath train. On the road above the station is the Great Western Hotel, from where liquid refreshments were taken by the passengers and crew of the last service train over the line later that day.

Access to the station from the road level above was provided via a stone-built stairway that survives to the present day, as does the masonry retaining wall at the back of the houses and bungalows that occupy the former railway land. *W. Potter/DCG*

QUAKER'S YARD (HIGH LEVEL) (2): On 12 June 1964 ex-GWR '5101' Class 2-6-2T No 4157 stands beneath the distinctive water tower at High Level station with the 1.00 pm Pontypool Road to Neath service. A portion of the lattice footbridge that enabled passengers access to the platforms of the Low Level station can just be seen behind the water tower.

Following closure of the line and subsequent clearance of the site, the land was sold for redevelopment. The view taken in May 1994 shows the roofs of private residences that now occupy the site. *W. Potter/DCG*

89

QUAKER'S YARD (HIGH LEVEL) (3): Upon leaving the High Level station the line to Neath swung west and immediately crossed the bridge that took it over the Taff Vale line. A short embankment followed, then the line crossed the viaduct over the River Taff before entering the 703-yard single-bore West Tunnel that took the railway beneath Bryn Glas to enter the Cynon Valley. On 12 June 1964 '5101' Class 2-6-2-T No 4169 approaches High Level Station with the 11.05 Neath to Pontypool Road service. The track in the foreground was once the alternative route to Merthyr that followed the west bank of the River Taff; as the Quaker's Yard & Merthyr Joint Line, it had been opened in April 1886 by the Great Western and Rhymney Railways in direct competition with the Taff Vale. A second viaduct took the Merthyr Joint Line across the valley just to the north of the Neath line, and mining subsidence required both structures to be strengthened by timber frameworks being placed in their arches. The unsafe nature of the Joint Line viaduct hastened the closure of this route in 1951, and both viaducts were eventually demolished in the 1960s.

Our view of February 1995 shows the considerable changes that have taken place in the intervening 30 years. The spoil tips above Bryn Glas have been reduced and re-profiled, and an expressway constructed along the west side of the valley has cut across the former Neath trackbed, although the location of the tunnel entrance is still visible. The trackbed of the former Joint Line is now occupied by the private gardens in the foreground. *W. Potter/DCG*

MOUNTAIN ASH (CARDIFF ROAD): On 18 April 1964 ex-GWR '9400' Class 0-6-0PT No 9488 arrives at Mountain Ash Cardiff Road from Aberdare shortly after midday. Immediately to the left of the footbridge and on the far side of the Cynon River can be seen the signal box and footbridge of the former Taff Vale Railway Mountain Ash Oxford Street station.

Our visit to the location in February 1995 found the site totally cleared. The gable end of the Nazareth Baptist Church on the right is decidedly more prominent in our present-day view and the road bridge that spans both the river and the still open Abercynon to Aberdare line and the buildings on the far side of the river provide a physical link between the pictures. A car park occupies the former station forecourt and a timber merchant the remainder of the station site. A short distance to the south of the site, the goods shed still survives in use by a local firm of builders merchants. *E. T. Gill/DCG*

ABERDARE (HIGH LEVEL): The single line from Gelli Tarw Junction to Aberdare had originally been opened as a branch by the Vale of Neath Railway in September 1851. The Aberdare Valley Railway Company opened a mineral-only line to serve Middle Duffryn Colliery in November 1857 and this in turn was to provide the connection with the line from Quaker's Yard in 1864. Amalgamation of the Vale of Neath with the Great Western Railway took effect in 1865. Our view of Aberdare High Level station on 11 May 1954 shows Class '5600' 0-6-2T No 6652 awaiting departure with the 3.45 service to Pontypool Road.

The station buildings survived the withdrawal of passenger services in 1964 and our view taken on 18 April 1993 of Class 37/7 No 37803 with the Cawoods Company coal containers service from Tower Colliery shows the buildings still standing, albeit in an abandoned and derelict state. More recently, the former GWR station buildings have been totally renovated to provide possible accommodation for a local business. *T. J. Edgington/B. Cole*

ABERDARE MPD: Coal mining in the Aberdare Valley was gathering momentum at the time that the Vale of Neath Railway opened its line in 1851, and by the following year there were 16 pits in production with a further 12 being developed. Coal therefore provided the foundation for the development and prosperity of the local railways. To cater for the motive power requirements of this substantial mineral traffic, the GWR opened its Aberdare shed in 1907, being a standard turntable unit shed introduced by G. J. Churchward. At nationalisation there was an allocation of 59 locomotives, the majority of which were employed hauling coal trains. Our view of the depot taken on 14 October 1962 shows a brace of '5600' Class locomotives, Nos 6622 and 5625, on the coaling stage road. The entrance to the roundhouse depot can be seen under the central gable. The repair shop, which was equipped with a 30-ton overhead crane, is on the left and the stores and office block on the right of the shed structure.

Closed on 1 March 1965, the shed was demolished and the land eventually cleared to permit construction of the business units that now occupy the site. *W. Potter/DCG*

GELLI TARW JUNCTION: On 13 October 1962 '5600' Class 0-6-2T No 6628 is provided with banking assistance by '2800' Class 2-8-0 No 3822 as it climbs up the 1 in 50 bank with a westbound freight from the Aberdare line. On the left the signalman offers the token to a Merthyr-bound service that will take the single line straight ahead. The line to Merthyr was the original main line of the Vale of Neath route and was opened from Gelli Tarw Junction on 2 November 1853. The line diverging to the right was opened in November 1854 to serve the collieries in the Dare Valley and was used for mineral traffic until it closed to traffic in September 1939.

The view of the former junction taken in May 1994 shows Class 56 No 56076 heading north with the MGR empties for loading at Tower Colliery. The trackbed of the former line to Merthyr is still clearly visible on the left. *John Dew/GPD*

HIRWAUN: The Vale of Neath Railway opened its double line from the junction with the South Wales Railway at Neath on 24 September 1851 as far as Hirwaun, with a single line continuing as far as Aberdare; passenger services to and from Merthyr via Gelli Tarw Junction commenced in November 1853. On 13 October 1962 '6400' Class push-pull-fitted 0-6-0PT No 6433 with trailer W342 forms the 2.35 to Merthyr Tydfil.

In May 1994 Class 56 No 56076 passes with a rake of empty HAA hoppers *en route* to Tower Colliery. Although the colliery had ceased production on 22 April, the clearance of coal stocks owned by National Power continued for a number of months. Fortunately, Tower Colliery, the last deep mine in South Wales, was re-opened in 1995 and in due course rail traffic may re-commence. *John Dew/DCG*

Past and Present Colour

South Wales
Part 1

CALDICOT HALT, on the main line from Gloucester near Severn Tunnel Junction, was a typical example of a GWR standard timber halt, large numbers of which were built from 1903 onwards to serve remote country communities. The lineside platforms were designed to be constructed cheaply and comprised a series of rectangular timber frames on which the platform, made up of planks, was laid. The corrugated iron 'Pagoda' shelter was another standard GWR architectural feature. Opened on 12 September 1932, Caldicot Halt survived the mass closures of the 1960s and continued to be served by the local trains that worked between Gloucester and Cardiff. Our April 1961 illustration shows the original timber-built Halt with an ex-GWR '2800' Class locomotive passing with a Gloucester-bound freight.

A visit to Caldicot on Friday 14 April 1995 was timed to record the arrival of Class 158 'Express' unit No 158 833 with the 0735 Milford Haven to Birmingham New Street. There is no timber or corrugated iron in the replacement structure now provided at Caldicot, with up-to-date style paved platforms and glazed shelters. *Alan Jarvis/Don Gatehouse*

NEWPORT HIGH STREET: A through passenger service off the Southern Region provides the subject of our view of Newport station on 23 March 1963, with '4900' 'Hall' Class No 6929 *Whorlton Hall* providing the customary motive power for such inter-regional passenger workings. On the right a '2800' Class locomotive approaches on the down through line with a westbound freight.

Class 158 'Express' units were introduced in South Wales in May 1991 and now provide the staple train formation on services to and from the South Coast of England. The corresponding view taken on Saturday 27 August 1994 shows No 158 818 setting off on the final leg of its journey to Cardiff Central with the 1024 from Portsmouth Harbour. *Alan Jarvis/Don Gatehouse*

PONTLLANFRAITH (LOW LEVEL) (1): Situated on the former Taff Vale Extension line that linked Pontypool Road with the Vale of Neath, Pontllanfraith saw considerable freight traffic during the steam era. On 27 July 1963 one of the versatile Churchward '4300' Class 2-6-0 mixed traffic locomotives, No 6361, approaches from Crumlin with a train of mineral wagons. This particular Churchward locomotive was one of a batch built at Swindon in 1923 and as such was not fitted with outside steam pipes and the side-window cab that was a feature of the later Collett-produced variants.

With the passage of nearly 32 years the corresponding view shows that part of the site is now used as a parking area for the nearby parish church. The recess in the embankment where the signal box stood can still be located amongst the undergrowth, and the track alignment to the left of the Church Hall is also visible. *Alan Jarvis/Geoff Dowling*

PONTLLANFRAITH (LOW LEVEL) (2): Our second illustration at this location on 27 July 1963 shows '5600' Class 0-6-2T No 5647 entering with a passenger service *en route* to Pontypool Road. Above the coaches of the train can be seen the back of the all-timber structure of Pontllanfraith High Level Station signal box, which controlled the level crossing situated at the southern end of the platforms. The road bridge that gave access to the railway crossing is visible to the rear of the train, and just beyond the road bridge is the railway bridge that took the Sirhowy Valley line over the Taff Vale Extension route.

The April 1995 view of the same location confirms the total transformation of the former railway alignment, with no visible trace of either the station, bridges or level crossing remaining. *Alan Jarvis/Geoff Dowling*

QUAKER'S YARD (HIGH LEVEL): On a sunny 31 March 1962 '5700' Class 0-6-0PT No 3685 arrives at Quaker's Yard (High Level) station with the late morning service from Aberdare (High Level) to Pontypool Road. The train was scheduled to cover the 23 miles in 67 minutes with 11 intermediate stops. At Quaker's Yard passengers from Merthyr Tydfil could connect with this service via the adjacent Low Level station.

The route across from Pontypool Road closed in June 1964 and our view of the same location exactly 30 years later shows no trace of the former railway, the land having been sold and redeveloped for private housing. Even the colliery spoil tips that once featured in the distance have been re-profiled to provide a more natural contour to the background hills. *Alan Jarvis/Don Gatehouse*

CRUMLIN (LOW LEVEL): A tramroad linking Beaufort Ironworks with the canal at Crumlin was opened in 1796, and some 60 years later it was converted to a standard gauge railway. With the original ironworks closed and superseded by steel production plants, imported iron ore had to be transported from Newport Docks up the Ebbw Valley for many decades. In 1954 the first of the British Railways Standard '9F' 2-10-0 locomotives were allocated to Newport Ebbw Junction specifically for this arduous work. It is therefore appropriate to illustrate both Crumlin and a train loaded with iron ore *en route* to Ebbw Vale Steelworks being banked by a BR '9F' in this view taken on 27 July 1963. Two of the slender pillars of Crumlin viaduct, which carried the Pontypool to Neath line 200 feet above the track level of the Western Valleys route, are also visible in the photograph.

With the establishment of steel plants on the coastal plain, the British Steel Corporation ceased production at Ebbw Vale, which then concentrated on the specialist work of producing tin plate and galvanised steel. Our view of the location in 1995 shows a trainload of steel coil from Llanwern heading up the valley in the care of Class 60 No 60093 *Jack Stirk*. *Alan Jarvis/Geoff Dowling*

LLANHILLETH: Viewed on 31 July 1963 from the road that follows the east side of the valley, the extent of the railway infrastructure that once served the Ebbw Vale is clearly illustrated. Above the short freight that is heading down the valley is Llanhilleth Steam Coal Colliery, and to the left can be seen Llanhilleth Branch Junction Middle Signal Box. The two tracks on the right lead to the single line that climbs up to join the Pontypool Road to Neath route at Crumlin Junction.

Unfortunately, the level of tree growth that had taken place in the intervening years prevented access for an exactly corresponding view, but the extent of the changes is all too evident when you compare the above illustration from the steam era with the March 1995 version. The elevated section of the A467 expressway overshadows the much rationalised railway, where Class 60 No 60033 *Samuel Johnson* is visible slowly threading its way up the valley with another consignment of steel coil for Ebbw Vale. *Alan Jarvis & Don Gatehouse*

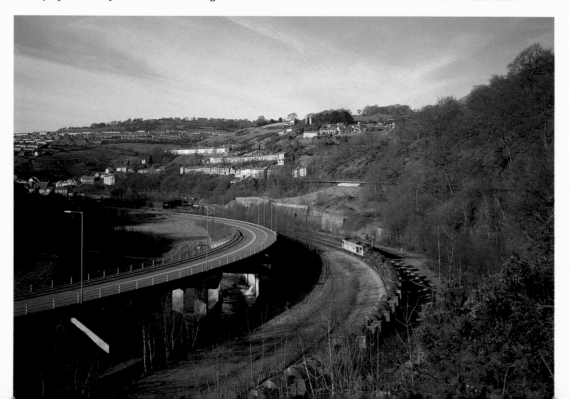

PONTLLANFRAITH (HIGH LEVEL): With the conversion from tramroad to railway completed in the 1860s to make an end-on connection with the Monmouthshire Railway at Nine Mile Point, a passenger service via Risca to Newport Dock Street commenced on 19 June 1865. Unfortunately, the passenger services over the former Sirhowy Valley line did not survive to celebrate their centenary and had ceased in June 1960. However, sections of the route continued to be used by what little freight traffic remained for a number of years thereafter, until the cessation of freight operations between Risca and Tredegar in May 1970. On 27 July 1963 a '5700' Class locomotive stands on the former up line at the north end of the then closed Pontllanfraith High Level station with a local freight working. Note that the tracks of the former down line in the foreground have been removed and weeds grow unchecked on the platforms.

Since the closure of the line local road developments have obliterated almost all trace of the former railway. However, our corresponding view taken in April 1995 shows the survival of a section of the old platform face beneath the trees that have now matured to shade the remains of the station site. *Alan Jarvis/ Geoff Dowling*

Lines to Merthyr Tydfil

LLWYDCOED: The Vale of Neath Railway opened its single line from Gelli Tarw Junction to Merthyr Tydfil on 2 November 1853. Work had begun in 1847 and it was the 2,495-yard Pencaedrain Tunnel that ran north-east some 650 feet beneath the summit of Mynydd Mawr to link the Cynon and Taff Valleys that was to take until August 1853 to complete. Llwydcoed was the only intermediate station when the route first opened. On 28 April 1962 ex-GWR '6400' Class 0-6-0PT No 6416 pauses at the station with a Merthyr auto-train.

Some 33 years later the site of the station is overgrown, although the platform formation is still in situ. The adjacent Station House and nearby Station Villas provide a reminder of their respective railway origins. *E. T. Gill/DCG*

ABERNANT was the second intermediate station on the line between Gelli Tarw Junction and Merthyr, opened in 1853. Our second view of the same evening auto-train service from Hirwaun on 28 April 1962 illustrates the additional and unconventional signage that was provided on the non-platform side of the line! This auto-train shuttle service provided a link between Merthyr Tydfil and the Pontypool to Neath line until the withdrawal of services from 31 December 1962.

The trackbed now forms the Llwycoed to Cwmbach Footpath along this section of the Cynon Valley for the use of walkers, ramblers and other leisure users, as illustrated in our April 1995 photograph. *E. T. Gill/GPD*

MERTHYR MPD: Originally opened in 1877, Merthyr MPD comprised a three-road dead-ended brick-built shed. In 1932 the shed building was extended, and at the same time a 55-foot turntable was installed, together with a covered coaling plant. When it passed into British Railways ownership the shed had an allocation of 20 locomotives, the majority of which were 0-6-0 Pannier tanks for use on local freight and passenger duties. On the day of a depot visit in May 1956 locomotives Nos 9618 and 4632 were visible in the shed, while No 9638 can be seen in front of the corrugated-iron-covered coaling plant, behind which was located the turntable.

Closed on 2 November 1964, the shed buildings saw industrial use for a number of years. The site was eventually sold for a housing development and at the time of our visit in February 1995, construction work at 'Trevethick Gardens' was well advanced. *W. Potter/GPD*

MERTHYR TYDFIL: The Taff Vale Railway (TVR) provided the first rail line to arrive at Merthyr in April 1841 and established its terminus at Plymouth Street. The Vale of Neath Railway established its terminus at High Street in 1853, and this latter terminus was also used by the Brecon & Merthyr Railway from 1868, the original broad gauge tracks having been converted for mixed gauge operation in 1864 and solely standard gauge in 1872. The TVR had diverted its services into High Street station from August 1877, by June 1879 the LNWR had established running powers over the B&M line, and finally in 1886 the Rhymney & GWR Joint line arrived from Quaker's Yard. The gauge conversion enabled an additional narrow timber platform to be built between the original arrival and departure platforms and this is clearly illustrated in this view taken on 30 August 1951, as is the original Brunel roof. Trains occupy the two arrival roads on the left and on the right 0-6-0PT No 7772 and 0-4-2T No 1425 wait with departures for Pontsticill and Hirwaun.

The original Brunel structure was eventually replaced by 1971, when new facilities were opened at the much rationalised station. On 14 April 1995 Class 143 'Pacer' unit No 143 603 awaits departure with the 13.50 service to Penarth via Cardiff. *Ian L. Wright/DCG*

CEFN COED: The Brecon & Merthyr Railway opened its branch from Pontsticill Junction to Rhydycar Junction on the former Vale of Neath line on 1 August 1868, from where running powers over the GWR permitted access to Merthyr Tydfil High Street station. A journey from Merthyr entailed a steep and continuous climb at a ruling gradient of 1 in 45, the railway making a clockwise spiral to the west of the town with the line carried on an embankment that was a long thin slag heap of quarrying and mining waste. The principal intermediate station on the line was at Cefn Coed, where crossing facilities were provided. Approaching from Merthyr, the railway was carried high across the Afon Taf Fawr Valley on a 15-arch, 770-foot-long viaduct. Completed in 1866, this superlative piece of 19th-century workmanship remains in situ and has been designated a Class II listed structure. On 27 April 1960 a Merthyr-bound auto-train calls at Cefn Coed.

The land once occupied by the main station building and goods shed is now occupied by a block of flats, with the former trackbed providing a footpath for local residents. *E. T. Gill/DCG*

PONTSARN HALT: Construction of the branch line had proved expensive for the B&M, although half of the costs were subsequently recouped from the LNWR when an agreement was reached between the two companies to construct a connection at Morlais Junction. This then allowed the LNWR to introduce through services from Abergavenny via the Heads of the Valleys line on 1 June 1879 and finally to reach Merthyr over what became the B&M & LNWR Joint Line. On 12 August 1961 Pannier tank No 6433 calls at Pontsarn with the 10.02 Pontsticill Junction to Merthyr service, being one of ten local services in each direction that would call at the Halt on a typical weekday.

Immediately north of the single platform, the line passed beneath the road bridge and then crossed the Taf Fechan on the Pontsarn viaduct. The platform formation is still in place and the former trackbed has been incorporated into the Taff Trail, which links Cardiff to Brecon and provides an idyllic way to walk or cycle through parts of the local countryside that were once viewed from a railway carriage. As with the Cefn Coed viaduct, the Pontsarn structure is also a listed monument. *A. F. Smith, Peter Rowe (Printers)/GPD*

Brecon & Merthyr Railway
(Northern Section)

FOCHRIW: From its end-on junction with the Rhymney Railway at Deri in the Bargoed Rhymney Valley, northbound trains over the Northern Section of the former B&M route faced an arduous 4-mile climb at a ruling gradient of 1 in 38/40 until the summit of the line was reached before Dowlais Top. At Fochriw, where a brief respite for locomotives could be obtained, a crossing loop was provided and the station had staggered platforms, the down platform being sited to the north of the up. A single siding serving the goods shed made a trailing connection with the up line. Our view of the main station buildings on the up platform was taken only a few days prior to the closure of the station on 31 December 1962, when both passenger and goods services ceased.

The line between Deri Junction and Pant Junction remained open for freight traffic until August 1963, and following closure the track was lifted. Although most traces of the former station have been removed with the passage of years, a section of the up platform was still in situ as seen in our corresponding view recorded in April 1995. *John Hodge/DCG*

PANTYWAEN: Travelling north from Fochriw to Dowlais the railway entered an area that was windswept and desolate, being scarred by former limestone pits and other reminders of the region's industrial heritage. On 9 May 1959 '5700' Class 0-6-0PT No 7736 was photographed climbing away from Fochriw on the ascent to Pantywaen Halt with the Saturdays-only 3 pm Newport to Brecon service. The train would have taken about 1 hour 25 minutes to complete its journey of 24 miles from Newport to this location and would soon reach the summit of the line at approximately 1,314 feet above sea level, prior to arriving at Dowlais Top. In 1959 the total journey time for the 47 miles from Newport to Brecon was 2 hours 35 minutes and included 21 intermediate stops *en route*.

Our visit to the location in April 1995 confirmed that the former track alignment was still visible to the south, with a waste disposal firm using the trackbed for the storage of skips. To the north of this location the former railway cutting has been subject to in-fill, and land reclamation further north has obliterated all trace of the former railway alignment. *R. O. Tuck/DCG*

DOWLAIS TOP: The Brecon & Merthyr Tydfil Railway Junction Railway opened the line from Pant to Dowlais Top on 1 August 1867, with the section to Deri Junction opening a year later. When the LNWR extended its Heads of the Valleys route westward to Dowlais in 1873, its line passed under the B&M route just to the east of Dowlais Top and a connecting spur was subsequently provided for the exchange of goods, mineral and occasional excursion traffic. On 27 April 1960 '5700' Class Pannier tank No 3662 of Newport Ebbw Junction shed (86A) enters with a Newport to Brecon service. A single siding for goods traffic was provided at the west end of the station, with goods facilities finally being withdrawn from 27 March 1961.

A visit to the former station site in April 1995 found it totally obliterated by a scrap yard, with only the profile of the distant hills providing a point of reference. Although traces of the B&M formation can be found on either side of the site, the nearby A465 trunk road has been built over the alignment of the LNWR Heads of the Valleys route. *E. T. Gill/DCG*

PANT (GLAM) (1): On 27 April 1960 ex-GWR '5700' Class 0-6-0PT No 4632 of Merthyr shed (88D) heads a lunchtime working from Dowlais Central to Bargoed. The short journey from Dowlais would have involved a stiff climb for much of the way at 1 in 80 with the final approach to Pant Junction at 1 in 40. Upon arrival at Pant, the locomotive would have run round the two coaches prior to drawing the train into one of the main platforms on the Brecon to Newport line. The main station building on the up platform is visible to the left of the locomotive; a small corrugated shelter was the only structure provided on the down platform.

In 1994 only the platforms survived in situ, all other structures having long since been demolished. *E. T. Gill/DCG*

PANT (GLAM) (2): The winter of 1962/63 was extremely harsh with many areas of the country gripped by the 'Great Winter Freeze' for many weeks. Our winter scene taken on 29 December 1962 shows ex-GWR '5700' Class 0-6-0PT No 4679 of Newport Ebbw shed (86A) taking water while working the 8.03 Newport to Brecon. Behind Pant Junction Signal Box was the single short platform on the Dowlais branch. Withdrawal of passenger and goods services came on 31 December 1962.

Our corresponding view taken in less severe conditions in the spring of 1994 shows only the trackbed area and platform formations to confirm the location of the former station. Just visible on the right of the picture is the main station of the Brecon Mountain Railway, from where services were introduced in June 1980 to Pontsticill. The narrow gauge railway operates steam-hauled trains from Pant between April and October, and the 7-mile round trip follows for the majority of its route the former trackbed of the B&M line. *Hugh Ballantyne/GPD*

PONTSTICILL JUNCTION station was opened on the Brecon & Merthyr main line on 1 August 1867 for services to and from Cefn Coed, with the Merthyr branch being completed and opened throughout for public services a year later. Our view of 5 September 1959 shows '2251' Class Collett 0-6-0 locomotive No 2287 of Brecon shed (89B) on the 2.05 Brecon to Newport service. These locomotives, together with the ubiquitous ex-GWR Pannier tanks, were the regular motive power for services on the route between Brecon and Newport.

Following the withdrawal of freight services and the final closure of the railway in 1964, the tracks were lifted and the station buildings fell into disrepair. In 1980 the narrow gauge Brecon Mountain Railway was built and in the following years both the station buildings and in particular the former Brecon & Merthyr Railway signal box have been restored for use as holiday accommodation. When visited in April 1995, the fine start to the Easter Bank Holiday weekend had brought many people to the Brecon Beacons National Park and a good number were enjoying the final leg of their 7-mile round trip on one of the steam-hauled trains. The railway had in fact opened a new extension of its line that month, with services now running the full length of the Taf Fechan Reservoir to Dol-y-Gaer. *Hugh Ballantyne/GPD*

DOWLAIS, IVOR JUNCTION: At Ivor Junction, down the branch to Dowlais Central, the line from Pant was joined by the short spur from Penywern Junction on the LNWR Heads of the Valleys line over which passenger and goods services had been introduced in June 1879. The view looking north through the narrow rock cutting taken on 6 May 1960 shows ex-GWR Pannier tank No 9618 standing on the line to Penywern Junction, with the line to Pant passing to the left of the signal box.

As was the case elsewhere along the Heads of the Valleys route, the construction of the A465 trunk road required land formerly used by the railway and, following track recovery, the Penywern spur was soon to disappear under the new road development. The elevated section of the A465 road is visible in the background of our view of the site taken in May 1994. The site is now used by the local Council as a highways maintenance depot for vehicle and equipment storage. *E. T. Gill/GPD*

DOWLAIS CENTRAL (1): Dowlais Lloyd Street (later Central) was the terminus of the short branch of the B&M from Pant, opened to both passenger and goods traffic on 23 June 1869. The station site had been formed on a tip created from waste from the Dowlais Ironworks and our view of the station area taken on 6 May 1960 shows '5700' Class 0-6-0PT No 9676 waiting to depart with the 12.58 service to Pant and Bargoed. Visible behind the single-road platform is the goods shed, and to the left is a short goods bay with cattle pens. Pannier tank No 4632 is just visible on the shed road on the right.

The corresponding view of May 1994 shows that the site is now used as a recreation area with both the former station building and goods shed still in situ. *E. T. Gill/DCG*

DOWLAIS CENTRAL (2): At only 1 mile 22 chains long, the Dowlais branch was one of the shortest that passed into British Railways ownership. There were eight return trips over the branch on weekdays and two additional ones on Saturdays, with 6 minutes being sufficient time for a single journey, including a stop at the intermediate Halt at Pantyscallog. The ordinary passenger services were withdrawn on 28 June 1952, although workmen's service trains continued to use the route and it was not until May 1960 that these services finally ceased. On 27 April 1960 Pannier tank No 4632 has just arrived with a train from Bargoed via Pant. The basic finish of the B&M station building rendered in cement is clearly visible on the right and gas lamps were still in place until closure. Goods traffic continued until May 1964.

Our view taken 30 years later shows that the building fabric has been refurbished and the site cleared and grassed for recreational purposes. *E. T. Gill/GPD*

DOWLAIS CENTRAL MPD: Our view taken on a wet 26 August 1951 shows the small brick-built shed at Dowlais Central constructed in 1916 to replace the original B&M structure erected in 1898 to house the Pant branch locomotive. When the shed passed into British Railways ownership it became a sub-shed to Merthyr and the allocation was initially the former Taff Vale Railway Class '04' locomotive No 292 (formerly No 58) illustrated here. Being one of a Class of 41 such 0-6-2T engines acquired by the GWR in 1922, this Beyer Peacock locomotive of 1908 vintage was later rebuilt at Swindon and fitted with a Standard No 3 tapered boiler.

The shed was closed in May 1960 and the building subsequently demolished to permit the site to be used for recreational purposes, as illustrated in our view taken in 1994. *W. Potter/DCG*

The Taff Bargoed line

DOWLAIS CAE HARRIS (1): The Taff Bargoed Joint Line was built by the GWR in partnership with the Rhymney Railway (RR) and was opened for freight traffic in January 1876. The objective of this joint venture was to access the then industrial boom town of Dowlais, where the furnaces of the ironworks required a constant supply of iron ore, much of which was imported. In addition to the significant tonnage of freight moved to and from Dowlais over the years, several collieries along the valley supplied revenue-earning coal traffic. The British Railways passenger timetable of the 1960s shows that a typical weekdays-only service over the line comprised five return trips between Dowlais and either Ystrad Mynach or Hengoed High Level, to connect with services on the Rhymney Valley line. The early morning and lunchtime departures from Dowlais Cae Harris and the respective return workings were designated workmen's trains. There were also two additional late evening return trips over the then route on Saturdays only. Passenger services ended on 13 June 1964 and our view of the station platform shows '5600' Class No 5662 waiting to depart for Ystrad Mynach.

There is no visible trace of the railway in our view of the site in the spring of 1994. The large white building in the centre of the frame is the structure visible behind the station building in the earlier illustration. *W. Potter/DCG*

DOWLAIS CAE HARRIS (2): Looking north over the station site on 10 June 1957, the Brecon Beacons can be seen in the distance. Waiting to depart with the 1.55 pm Saturdays-only service to Ystrad Mynach is '5600' Class 0-6-2T No 5602. In the left foreground is Cae Harris shed, opened in 1876 and constructed of stone with a slated roof and timber gables. In British Railways ownership it was a sub-shed to Merthyr Tydfil and the allocation comprised half a dozen of the versatile ex-GWR 0-6-2 tanks. A coaling platform was originally sited in front of the water tank in the right foreground, but this had been demolished when the coaling facilities beneath the corrugated steel awning, visible in front of the shed, were added in the mid-1950s.

The shed closed in December 1964 and in due course all of the railway infrastructure and buildings were demolished. The land was later re-profiled and, by studying our corresponding view of 1994, several of the buildings to the rear of the former station site can be matched with the earlier illustration. On the extreme right of the picture is the former station house of the LNWR's Dowlais High Street station. *E. T. Gill/GPD*

116

CWMBARGOED: Between Taff Bargoed Junction and Cwmbargoed the line climbs at between 1 in 40 and 49 for nearly 7 miles. At the summit of the climb was the remote station of Cwmbargoed and it is here on 18 April 1964 that '5600' Class No 5602 pauses with an Ystrad Mynach to Dowlais Cae Harris train. On the left sister locomotive No 6612 stands on the branch from Fochriw Colliery with a train of loaded mineral wagons. Fixed on the lamp bracket above the right-hand front buffer is the metal disc that displays the 'target' number KO5. This identified the starting point of the particular working, K being the letter code for Dowlais Cae Harris with the number denoting the particular engine diagram.

Just over 30 years later, on 7 August 1994, Class 37/7 No 37898, appropriately named *Cwmbargoed DP*, arrives with a train of empty coal hoppers from Barry High Level Sidings. The locomotive will run round the wagons before taking them up the line to the left of the locomotive to access the loading facilities at the open-cast coal disposal point that is visible in the background above the coal hoppers. The earth mound on the right is the only remnant of the former station platform. *E. T. Gill/GPD*

BEDLINOG: Approximately halfway up the ascent of the Taff Bargoed Valley lies the remote community of Bedlinog. Following a landslide near Taff Merthyr in 1952 the down line through Bedlinog was taken out of use and, by the time of our view of the closed station, taken on 31 July 1965, the line had been singled throughout. On the day in question the 'Rambling 56' rail tour visited a number of lines in the area and motive power was provided by '5600' Class 0-6-2T No 6643.

An empty MGR working from Aberthaw to Cwmbargoed hauled by Trainload Coal-liveried Class 37/7 locomotives Nos 37897 and 37799 provides the subject of the corresponding illustration captured on Tuesday 4 May 1993. The station site had been reduced to a mound of earth and rubble, but the Station Hotel was still open for business; alas, even that has since closed and was seen empty and boarded up some two years later. *W. Potter/DCG*

118

NELSON & LLANCAIACH: Here the Taff Bargoed services connected with trains for either Pontypool Road or Neath. On 28 December 1963 ex-GWR '5600' Class No 6612 waits at the Dowlais platform with the lunchtime Ystrad Mynach to Cae Harris service, providing a connection with the 10.30 Swansea High Street to Pontypool Road working that would arrive at the adjacent platform. Within six months of the date of our photograph the station had closed to passenger trains. The signal box visible in the background remained operational for a further four years before it too closed and was demolished.

The platform formation, although cut back and now overgrown, has survived the passage of time and provided the same vantage point from which to record Class 37/7 Nos 37897 and 37797 ambling through with a train of empty HAA coal hoppers *en route* to Cwmbargoed on Friday 14 April 1995. *Hugh Ballantyne/GPD*

YSTRAD MYNACH: At Taff Bargoed Junction trains joined the GWR line from Neath to Pontypool. A short distance further east access to and from the Rhymney main line was made via a short spur from Penallta Junction to Ystrad Mynach, where platforms were provided on the spur adjacent to the RR's station to cater for passenger traffic along the route. On 31 August 1957 ex-RR 0-6-2T locomotive No 36 takes the line leading up to Penallta Junction with the 'target' D3 trip working to Tredomen. Revenue-earning freight is also the theme of our corresponding view of the location taken on Sunday 5 May 1994, with Class 37/7 No 37899 heading 6C05, the 0810 Barry High Level to Cwmbargoed MGR working. Note the remaining overgrown platform on the right.
R. O. Tuck/DCG

The Western Valleys

GAER JUNCTION, NEWPORT: Opened on 1 January 1879, the loop between Gaer and Park junctions enabled Western Valleys trains to access the enlarged High Street Station in Newport following its opening in March 1880. This post-war illustration of a typical Sirhowy Valley train formation shows ex-LNWR 'Coal Tank' No 7834 on a Tredegar to Newport train comprising a pair of LMS Stanier coaches and an ex-Lancashire & Yorkshire coach at the rear. The line to Park Junction climbs away to the right before entering Gaer Tunnel. Above the roof line of the coaches, the connections between the former Relief and Main lines that enabled passenger trains to swing over either to or from the main platforms at Newport High Street station can be seen.

The 1994 view of the junction was much hindered by vegetation as 'Express Sprinter' unit No 158 823 passed with a Regional Railways service from Cardiff Central. *J. Hubback, courtesy of John Hodge/GPD*

PARK JUNCTION: The railways of the Western Valleys were developed from the series of canals and tramroads that had been constructed from the late 18th century onwards by the Monmouthshire Railway & Canal Company (MRCC) to link Newport Docks with the Beaufort Ironworks at Ebbw Vale and Coalbrook Vale Ironworks near Nantyglo. Access to Newport was through Tredegar Park, and the owner, Sir Charles Morgan, was entitled to take tolls for the passage of goods along what became known as the 'Park Mile' or 'Golden Mile'. From 1805 until 1922, when the GWR bought out the family interest, tolls were extracted from every ton of minerals that passed along this section of railway, which at its peak of operation comprised six tracks. Park Junction marked the southern end of the 'Golden Mile' and at the time of our photograph, 3 September 1956, the four tracks of the former GWR route were still in situ, as were the two lines of the former Alexandra Dock Railway that lay on the far side of the signal box. Our view shows an ex-GWR '4200' Class 2-8-0 tank passing the signal box, with a '5700' Class Pannier tank at the head of a Tredegar to Newport train about to take the line down to Gaer Junction.

The signal box at Park Junction now controls traffic movements between the South Wales main line and either the Western Valleys route to Ebbw Vale or the remaining section of the former B&M line as far as Machen Quarry, from where rail ballast is supplied. On 14 April 1995 Class 60 No 60065 *Kinder Low* takes the line down to the Cardiff Curve with the morning steel empties from Ebbw Vale to Margam. *S. C. L. Phillips/GPD*

BASSALEG: Conversion of the tramroads to railways in the Western Valleys was completed in 1855 and at Bassaleg Junction the Western Valleys line was joined by the Brecon & Merthyr Railway route when the latter company began running passenger trains into Newport in December 1864. With Bassaleg Junction station visible in the background, ex-GWR '5700' Class 0-6-0PT No 4611 heads a northbound train comprising a variety of empty open wagons on 15 February 1954. The train is heading for the yard at Rogerstone, which until its closure in 1968 served as the principal marshalling yard for traffic in the Western Valleys.

The view of 9 May 1995 at least confirms that the route is still open for freight traffic, albeit as a single line. Class 60 No 60015 *Bow Fell* heads north with a train of steel coil from Margam to Ebbw Vale. *John Hodge/DCG*

RISCA: The MRCC line from Risca to Nine Mile Point was completed as a goods railway by November 1855, but it was not until 1865, when running powers were obtained by the Sirhowy Railway, that passenger services commenced. On 28 May 1960 ex-GWR '6400' Class 0-6-0PT No 6426 is seen approaching Risca Junction from the Sirhowy branch with an auto-train. The Western Valley lines to Aberbeeg curve away to the right.

Passenger services between Risca and Nantybwch ceased in June 1964, but final closure of the line from Bird-in-Hand near Pontllanfraith to Risca Junction for mineral traffic did not occur until May 1970. With the station site at Risca long since cleared and the station footbridge demolished, the corresponding elevated vantage point could not be achieved when the location was visited in April 1995. Prior to the 1992 Ebbw Vale Garden Festival a study was conducted as part of a scheme to re-establish passenger services between Newport and the larger centres of population in the Western Valleys. Unfortunately, the various options were rejected on the grounds of cost, and towns like Risca must continue to rely on road transport alone despite having a freight-only line that supports a handful of train movements each day passing through. *E. T. Gill/GPD*

ABERBEEG (1): The station at Aberbeeg was situated in the fork of the lines that continued either north-west to Ebbw Vale or north-east to Abertillery, and through to Nantyglo. The main road high above the station on the east side of the valley provides an excellent vantage point from where railway activity could be observed, and on 7 November 1963 an iron ore working from Newport Docks to Ebbw Vale thunders through the station with a brace of the recently delivered English Electric Type 3 diesel-electric locomotives (later Class 37) providing the train and banking motive power. The tracks to Abertillery are visible in the bottom right of the picture.

With the opening of the Llanwern Steelworks in 1962, the British Steel Corporation was able to cease steel production at the Ebbw Vale site, so the flow of iron ore up the valley was in due course superseded by the movement of rolled steel coil for the production of tin plate and galvanised steel. Our corresponding view of March 1995 shows Class 60033 *Anthony Ashley Cooper* heading towards Ebbw Vale with a consignment of steel coil. *R. O. Tuck/GPD*

ABERBEEG (2): On 23 April 1962 the 2.33 DMU shuttle service from Ebbw Vale has just arrived at Aberbeeg station. Most of the Western and Eastern Valleys passenger services from Newport went over to diesel multiple unit operation from 1958, and in June 1961 proposals for the withdrawal of passenger services were published; this was accomplished from 30 April 1962.

Freight flows to and from the former steelworks and latterly the tin plate works at Ebbw Vale have ensured a continued viability for the line up the Ebbw Fawr, and the delivery of hot rolled coil from the BSC plants at Margam and Llanwern is scheduled to be undertaken on six days of the week. On Sunday 1 May 1994 Class 60 No 60062 *Samuel Johnson* glides through the former station with 6B82, the 1440 Llanwern to Ebbw Vale Trainload Freight Metals working. *Michael Mensing/GPD*

ABERBEEG MPD: Opened in 1919, Aberbeeg shed was sited about a mile south of the station on the west side of the running lines. Originally a sub-shed to Ebbw Vale, it had gained parent shed status during the Second World War. At nationalisation the locomotive allocation was 37, comprising in the main motive power for freight and mineral traffic. The main brick-built depot comprised a standard Churchward four-road dead-end shed with office accommodation along the entire length of the east side of the building. Our 'past' illustration was taken at the time of a depot visit on 14 October 1962.

Closed in December 1964, the buildings have been incorporated into a brass foundry, and our view of May 1994 shows the original MPD structure as a core element of the industrial premises. *W. Potter/GPD*

MARINE COLLIERY, CWM: The Marine Pits at Cwm in the Ebbw Fawr were completed to a depth of 414 yards in 1891 by the Ebbw Vale Steel Iron & Coal Company Limited. Production and the workforce increased during the early part of this century, the latter reaching a peak figure of 2,728 in 1919. Marine Colliery platforms did not appear in the public timetable, and until 2 October 1961 a workmen's service from Beaufort near Ebbw Vale was provided. From 1977 underground connections allowed coal from the Six Bells Pit (Abertillery) to be brought to the surface at Cwm and the combined annual output of 650,000 tons in 1986 saw the complex provide much of the coal required by BSC Llanwern. On 22 September 1983 Class 37 No 37266 passes the site of the former up platform with a train of empty HTV coal wagons arriving from Llanwern steelworks.

Unfortunately, geological faults hindered production in the late 1980s and closure of the colliery was announced in January 1989. Rail connections were soon removed and demolition of the colliery site followed. Our corresponding view of 18 April 1993 illustrates the thoroughness with which the former colliery sites was cleared, with only the locations of the former pit shafts marked in appropriate fashion. The Llanwern BSC to Ebbw Vale steel train is in the care of one of the refurbished Class 37/7 variants, No 37801. The locomotive carries the former Coal Sector livery and by this time had lost its *Aberthaw* nameplates. *Both GPD*

ROSE HEYWORTH COLLIERY: The branch from Aberbeeg north through Abertillery had its origins as a tramroad opened in 1824 to connect the Coalbrook Ironworks between Blaina and Nantyglo with the Beaufort Tramroad at Aberbeeg. Passenger services had operated in tramroad days, prior to the conversion by the MRCC to a standard gauge railway in 1855. Passenger services were extended from Blaina to Nantyglo in 1858 and from the latter location to Brynmawr on the Heads of the Valleys route in 1906. On 23 April 1962 the 3.15 Newport to Brynmawr DMU passes the Rose Heyworth Colliery just to the south of Bournville Halt. Passenger services were withdrawn a week later and it was left to the coal production of the Ebbw Fach collieries to maintain rail activity on the line for a further decade until closure north of Blaina was completed by November 1973. The line was further cut back to Rose Heyworth in July 1976 and final closure came in 1983, when coal traffic had ceased.

Little remains to trace the course of the railway along the valley as the construction of the A467 trunk road has in the main obliterated the former trackbed. Our visit in 1995 also found no obvious trace of the colliery, but the nearby Rose Heyworth Business Park, a project part financed by the European Regional Development Fund, provides a reminder at least in title of the location's industrial heritage.
Michael Mensing/DCG

132

VICTORIA: Meanwhile, back on the Ebbw Vale line, the Victoria Ironworks had opened in 1837 and given its name to the local community situated immediately south of the town of Ebbw Vale. In this photograph the southern end of the British Steel complex dominates the scene behind the 1.35 pm Ebbw Vale to Aberbeeg DMU service photographed approaching Victoria station on 23 April 1962. The rail facilities at nearby Waunllwyd acted as the exchange yard for BSC Ebbw Vale until 1988, when extensive work was carried out in preparation for the 1992 Garden Festival. A new set of exchange sidings were provided about half a mile further north of the Waunllwyd site and were opened on 2 January 1989. It is these exchange sidings that now feature in the corresponding view taken on Sunday 12 March 1995 as Class 60 No 60033 *Anthony Ashley Cooper* arrives with a train-load of steel coil from Margam. *Michael Mensing/GPD*

EBBW VALE (LOW LEVEL) was the destination for Western Valley passenger services up the Ebbw Fawr and comprised a single platform. Examination of the passenger timetable of the early 1960s shows an approximately hourly service on weekdays between Ebbw Vale and Aberbeeg, where a connection was made with the Newport to Brynmawr services. On 23 April 1962 the 1.35 service to Aberbeeg awaits departure. The line to the left of the DMU continued north for a further 52 chains to Beaufort from where workmen's trains were provided until October 1961.

Our view of the site taken some 33 years later betrays little evidence of the former railway, the station site having been cleared completely and a road occupying the former trackbed. The stone retaining wall is still in situ in the bottom left-hand corner of the frame, and the buildings to the right provide a physical link between the two illustrations.
Michael Mensing/DCG

Brecon & Merthyr Railway (Southern Section)

MACHEN: The southern section of the Brecon & Merthyr Tydfil Junction Railway (B&M) had its origins in a tramroad known as the 'Old Rumney'. Originally incorporated in May 1825, the tramroad was to provide a link from the Rhymney Ironworks along the east side of the Rhymney Valley, then eastwards to Bassaleg where it joined the Monmouthshire Tramroad to Newport. With a view to upgrading the route the Rumney Railway Company was incorporated in August 1861, but the B&M purchased the Old Rumney on 28 July 1863. The reconstruction work was completed to enable passenger services to commence between Pengam and Newport (Dock Street) in June 1865. At Machen the B&M had established its engine works and carriage repair depot, and in due course the Caerphilly branch joined just beyond the west end of the platforms. This view of the station taken in 1954 shows auto-fitted 0-6-0PT No 6402 about to propel its train from the down to the up platform road prior to departing for Caerphilly and Pontypridd.

Part of the B&M line survives for the supply of railway ballast from Powell Duffryn's Quarry at Machen, but this is to the east of the station site and our 1994 visit merely confirmed the inevitable advance of vegetation. The station building was still in use, however, as a store for a local vending machine business.
Rev R. W. A. Jones/DCG

TRETHOMAS: From the junction with the GWR at Bassaleg, northbound trains would face an almost continuous climb westwards into the Rhymney Valley. Between Trethomas and Bedwas there were four tracks to provide relief lines for coal trains, and there were a number of works sidings including those serving Bedwas Navigation Colliery and the British Benzol Coke Works. Trethomas station had opened in 1915 in connection with the nearby colliery development and our view taken on 15 November 1963 shows '5700' Class No 4627 shunting wagons at the adjacent coke works. Passenger services had been withdrawn at the end of 1962 but the section to Bedwas Colliery remained open.

The goods yard at Trethomas was closed in July 1964, by which time the line from Machen had been singled and was worked as a siding. The pit closures of the mid-1980s saw an end of production at Bedwas and the final closure and recovery of track along this section of the B&M. Visiting the site in 1994 we discovered the platform formations still in situ and the spoil tips dominating the skyline a physical reminder of the bygone coal-mining era. *R. L. Masterman/DCG*

BEDWAS: On 9 May 1959 0-6-0PT No 3767 of Brecon shed (89B) re-starts the 11.15 Newport to Brecon service away from Bedwas station. Of note is the Saxby & Farmer somersault signal sited on the up platform. To the right of the station site is the goods yard, which survived beyond the withdrawal of passenger services to close in April 1965.

The goods yard land was eventually sold for housing development, leaving only the former trackbed to return to nature. The cottages of Railway Terrace provide a lasting reminder of the B&M's passage along this section of the Rhymney Valley. *R. O. Tuck/DCG*

MAESYCYMMER: The B&M service was extended from Pengam to Rhymney on 16 April 1866. Two years later, the connection was made via Aberbargoed Junction that took the B&M across the Rhymney Valley to connect up with Rhymney Railway at Bargoed South Junction. With running powers established on the 2 miles 48 chains to Deri Junction, the link was finally completed between the 'Rumney' or Southern Section and the 'Brecon' or Northern Section. The Brecon & Merthyr retained its independence until, under the Railways Act of 1921, it was absorbed as a subsidiary of the Western Group (GWR) from 1 July 1922. Our 1962 photograph, taken from the north end of the up platform at Maesycymmer, shows a '5700' Class Pannier tank approaching from Pengam. The train is passing beneath Hengoed viaduct, an impressive 15-arch masonry structure built to carry the Taff Vale Extension line across the Rhymney Valley. Maesycymmer station was about half a mile from the stations at Hengoed on the west side of the valley.

Passenger services from Newport to Brecon and New Tredegar were withdrawn on 31 December 1962. The site of the former station at Maesycymmer was eventually cleared and our corresponding view of April 1994 illustrates the transformation. Hengoed viaduct survives as an industrial monument and beneath one of the arches can be seen the remains of the severed trackbed of the former B&M line. *R. L. Masterman/DCG*

NEW TREDEGAR (1): When first opened, the B&M's Rhymney branch was single track. In 1904 most of the branch was doubled and the opening of a number of collieries along the route saw a considerable growth in the coal traffic. Following a major landslide at New Tredegar Colliery on 11 April 1930, the upper portion of the branch was abandoned and passenger services were cut back to New Tredegar station. In this view looking south on 16 May 1952, '5700' Class 0-6-0PT No 3714 arrives with a train from Newport.

The changed profile of the hills on the right of our April 1995 view illustrates the extent of the work being undertaken in the Rhymney Valley to reduce the size of the colliery spoil tip at nearby Bargoed. *R. C. Riley/DCG*

NEW TREDEGAR (2): Through services to Newport from New Tredegar were provided each weekday morning with corresponding return workings in the late afternoon. In addition to the rather spartan service provided on the branch during a typical weekday, several workmen's trains were operated. This view looking north at New Tredegar on 6 May 1960 shows '5700' Class 0-6-0PT No 4671 with an afternoon workmen's train that will run to Machen for the convenience of the miners at Bedwas Colliery. At Machen the coaches will be detached, and the locomotive and brake van (visible at the rear of the coaches) will continue light to Newport.

The stone chapel of 1860 vintage still overlooks the former station site, which was used to provide a children's play area following the removal of the railway infrastructure. *E. T. Gill/GPD*

WATERLOO HALT: The single-track branch between Machen and Caerphilly was opened by the B&M in 1864 primarily to serve local collieries. However, the development of Newport as a coal shipping port in competition with Cardiff saw the branch assume greater strategic importance and in 1884 the first trains of coal from the Rhondda began to use the route. The steep climb of 1 in 39 encountered by eastbound loaded coal trains was a source of considerable operational difficulty and in order to assist the passage of the greatly increased levels of traffic, the more easily graded Machen loop line was constructed and brought into use in September 1891. The original B&M branch henceforth was used by westbound trains only, and when local passenger services commenced in 1905 a Halt was provided at Waterloo to serve as the up line equivalent of the Halt opened at Fountain Bridge a quarter

of a mile away on the down (eastbound) line. On 9 June 1964, a month prior to the closure of the former B&M line, ex-GWR '5600' Class 0-6-2T No 6658 approaches Waterloo with a train of empty mineral wagons *en route* to Tondu.

Although the railway had been abandoned for almost 30 years, the corresponding view taken in 1994 clearly shows the former railway cutting. *R. L. Masterman/DCG*

FOUNTAIN BRIDGE HALT: The single-line Machen loop via Fountain Bridge was opened in order to provide loaded coal trains heading for Newport with a more easily graded route at 1 in 200. The opening of the new line also saw the introduction of through passenger services in September 1891, but it was not until 1905 that the Halt at Fountain Bridge was opened. Our 1955 view of auto-fitted locomotive No 6438 arriving with a Pontypridd to Machen service clearly illustrates the basic facilities provided. The extent of the Halt is marked by the two sleepers set parallel to the running line and in front of the nameboard and oil lamp. To the left of the nameboard is a second oil lamp facing in the direction of approaching trains to assist the driver in locating the Halt after dark. Also note that the locomotive displays the Abercynon 'target' JE on the white disc mounted above the buffer beam, as this service was part of the daily duties of the Abercynon-based engine. British Railways weekday services along this unidirectional route comprised a morning and afternoon working between Pontypridd and Machen, with a corresponding late evening working on Saturdays only, a single late morning service from Pontypridd through to Newport and an early evening working from Caerphilly to Machen.

Passenger services were withdrawn in September 1956, although the route was used by freight trains for a number of years, with final closure between Caerphilly East and Machen junctions coming in November 1967. With the track lifted, the advance of nature has seen the site revert to forest and a visit in April 1994 was required prior to a fresh growth of leaves and vegetation to find what trace of the railway could be found. Remarkably, the remains of the well-rotted Halt sleepers were located and, close by in the undergrowth, was a former lineside concrete bin full of unused ballast! *Rev R. W. A. Jones/DCG*

The Sirhowy Valley

BLACKWOOD: With the development of ironworks in the Tredegar area, the Sirhowy Tramroad was constructed in the early years of the 19th century to convey materials to the wharves at Newport. Wagons were originally horse-drawn, but steam traction had arrived by 1830. The first pit in the area was Dukes Pit and coal was
raised initially in 1806. There then followed a rapid development of iron, coal and brick production in the valley. Conversion to a railway was undertaken in the 1860s and the Sirhowy Railway Company completed its line
to make an end-on connection with the Monmouthshire Railway at Nine Mile Point. Running powers over the
latter company's metals were granted and passenger services to Newport Dock Street commenced on 19 June
1865. Between 1875 and 1891 the Sirhowy line was doubled to cater for the increasing volumes of coal traffic.
The station at Blackwood was sited to the north of the town centre and originally had staggered platforms, with
timber-built extensions being added at a later date. This view looking north is dated 28 May 1960 and shows
the No 2 signal box, which was of standard LNWR design with a panelled brick base. The line in the bottom
left-hand corner of the picture
once gave access to New Rock
Colliery.

The April 1995 view gives no
visible evidence of the former station remains and only the houses
in the distance provide a physical
link between the two illustrations.
E. T. Gill/DCG

HOLLYBUSH: Situated about half a mile south of the original Sirhowy Railway station, which was adjacent to the Hollybush Colliery, the later LNWR-built station provided watering facilities on both the up and down roads. On a bright afternoon in May 1960 the auto-train bound for Risca drifts to a halt at Hollybush with Pannier tank No 6426 providing the motive power. The down platform was built along a steep river bank and was an all-timber construction of standard LNWR design.

At the north end of the up platform, beyond the footbridge, stood the brick-built station building, which has survived to this day and is now in private ownership. The brick-faced up platform is also a surviving feature in our May 1994 view. However, the timber structures on the former down side have long since disappeared and the embankment had returned to nature. *E. T. Gill/DCG*

TREDEGAR (1): On 13 July 1876 the Sirhowy Railway was taken over by the London & North Western Railway. The LNWR soon replaced the original station buildings at Tredegar with its own timber-built version, which in turn were replaced with a more substantial brick structure by the LMS in 1932. All passenger trains used the single long platform. This view of the southern end of the station taken from the coaling stage on 4 April 1960 shows the locomotive shed on the left. Built by the LNWR to replace the earlier Sirhowy Railway shed, it was originally a sub-shed to Abergavenny and had an allocation of 25 locomotives at the Grouping. Closure came on the same day as the withdrawal of passenger services and for many years the buildings stood in a semi-derelict state. The

146

rake of coaches stabled on the right includes ex-Burry Port & Gwendraeth Valley vehicles of 1939 vintage. The severely restricted loading gauge of the BPGV necessitated the building of seven such coaches 18 inches lower than standard and 3 inches narrower in overall width. After the withdrawal of passenger services on the BPGV in 1953 the coaches were transferred elsewhere in South Wales, in this case to Tredegar where the stock was used on local colliers' trains.

The corresponding view of May 1994 shows fresh tarmac in the foreground and across the site of the now demolished shed buildings to provide an access drive to the new by-pass road construction site. *E. T. Gill/DCG*

TREDEGAR (2): On the final day of passenger services, 11 June 1960, Pannier tank No 3634 stands at the north end of the platform with trailer W173W. In the background No 8711 backs up with additional coaches to be attached to go on to Nantybwch. This pair of locomotives and the stock later formed the final service train over the line.

In May 1994 the station buildings were still extant, although derelict. However, demolition soon followed as the site was being finally cleared for the road construction scheme. *Hugh Ballantyne/GPD*

SIRHOWY: Originally the northern terminus of the Sirhowy Railway, a steeply graded 2-mile extension north to join the Merthyr and Abergavenny line at Nantybwch was opened to the public on 2 November 1868. Sirhowy station then became the only crossing place on the single line between Tredegar and Nantybwch. The modest station buildings represented the later LNWR version, with horizontal rustic boarding, which superseded the earlier style employing vertical boarding. On a sunny 28 May 1960 '6400' Class 0-6-0PT No 6426 arrives with a train for Nantybwch and provides an idyllic scene of a bygone era.

The station site is now occupied by the Tredegar Ambulance Station. *E. T. Gill/GPD*

OAKDALE COLLIERY: On the east side of the Sirhowy Valley a second tramroad was completed in 1814 that linked the Manmoel area to the Monmouthshire Western Valley Tramroad to the north of Risca. Conversion of the northern section of the tramroad to a standard gauge railway as far as Penar Junction on the Taff Vale Extension line was completed in March 1886. Oakdale Colliery (named after a local wood) was one of the Sirhowy Valley pits served by this branch line, which was extended to Markham Colliery when it was sunk in 1912. Between 1927 and 1939 passenger services were operated on the line, but in British Railways ownership it was operated purely as a mineral railway. The two mining shafts at Oakdale reached over 2,000 feet below ground and during the 1980s considerable investment was made in the colliery, which saw underground connections made with both Markham and Celynen North pits. Output by up to five trains each day saw coal taken to the BSC plants at both Llanwern and Scunthorpe. Our view of the southern end of the colliery site on 15 May 1983 shows Class 37 No 37232 at the head of a train of loaded MDV wagons awaiting departure for Llanwern.

The line north of Oakdale had closed in 1986, when output from Markham Colliery ceased. In the summer of 1989 came the sudden announcement that Oakdale was to close, and when production ceased soon afterwards the era of deep mining in the Gwent Coalfield came to an end. Removal of the railway infrastructure soon followed, with track being recovered for re-use in the Taff Bargoed Valley. The colliery site was cleared and our view of May 1995 shows only the former train control board surviving as a clue to the site's former use. *Both GPD*

Newport to Marshfield

HILLFIELD TUNNEL: Situated just to the west of Newport High Street station, the original Hillfield Tunnel had a bore 742 yards in length and was the only tunnel on the South Wales Railway main line when it opened 1850. When the Relief lines were added in 1912 the second bore of 762 yards was cut, and it is from the western portal of this latter tunnel that GWR 'Hall' Class 4-6-0 No 5956 *Horsley Hall* emerges with a down freight train of open timber wagons in this delightful post-war illustration.

Operational changes made in the early 1960s saw the Main and Relief lines change sides through the tunnels, and our 29 April 1994 view of the site shows HST power car No 43177 at the head of the 1300 London Paddington to Swansea service gathering speed following its call at Newport. The introduction of HST services began with the Western Region timetables of October 1976, and in the following January there were 11 'InterCity 125' services in each direction between Paddington and Swansea. These front-line passenger train units now provide an approximate journey time of 1 hour 40 minutes for the 133½ miles from Paddington to Newport at an hourly frequency. *J. Hubback, courtesy of John Hodge/GPD*

GAER JUNCTION: Our second view from the post-war era illustrates some of the extensive array of timber-posted semaphore signals that once controlled movements at Gaer Junction. An LMS Stanier 2-8-0 '8F' locomotive passes on an up freight comprising timber open wagons loaded with various grades of coal.

The Newport area re-signalling scheme of the early 1960s saw the closure of Gaer Junction signal box and the removal of all of the associated semaphore signalling. On Thursday 7 July 1988 Class 08 diesel shunter No 08785 ambles past with a brake van having completed a day's shunting at the nearby Alexandra Dock Junction Yard. The sorting sidings at Alexandra Dock Junction have seen a variety of operations over the years, having served as principal freight yard for Newport until the early 1970s, to see a decline to virtual closure in 1984. Since then civil engineering trains and latterly Railfreight Distribution (RfD) activities have maintained an operation presence at the yard. *J. Hubback, courtesy of John Hodge/DCG*

NEWPORT, EBBW JUNCTION MPD: The Western Valleys line from Park Junction joins the South Wales main line via the Cardiff Curve at Ebbw Junction, which is opposite the west end of the marshalling sidings of Alexandra Dock Junction Yard. This proved to be an ideal location for the GWR to build its largest motive power depot in South East Wales. Opened in July 1915, Newport Ebbw was constructed to the standard Churchward design that included a double roundhouse shed, coaling stage and various other amenities with a large repair shop adjoining the main shed. Being the principal motive power depot of the Newport Division of the GWR system in South Wales, it had substantial provision for the repair of locomotives. Having the status of a Divisional repair shop, the facilities were not only used for the repair of its own allocation but also locomotives based at other sheds in the Division that did not require to be taken to the main works at Swindon. At nationalisation over 140 locomotives were allocated to the depot, the majority of which were employed in the haulage of freight trains. Originally coded NPT by the GWR, the shed allocation was re-coded 86A under British Railways ownership. Closure came in October 1965 and this scene taken in May of that year shows ex-GWR '5600' Class 0-6-2T No 6685 at the head of a forlorn collection of tank locomotives in front of the round-

house buildings. The coaling stage is visible to the right of the loco-motive's smokebox and in the background is the repair shop.

Following closure, the majority of the former railway land was cleared and a housing development now occupies the site. *W. Potter/DCG*

154

EBBW JUNCTION: With the introduction of diesel traction in South Wales, new depots were established at strategic locations, and Ebbw Junction provided the home base for an allocation of locomotives for the Newport area. On 26 February 1977 BR Class 45 No 45020, with steam-heating boiler operational, passes Ebbw Junction diesel depot where some of the allocation of Class 37 locomotives was on view. The depot did not survive operationally for many years, being closed as a servicing point in October 1982, when its work was transferred to Severn Tunnel Junction. The site continued to be used as a locomotive stabling point until late 1983, when the depot site was vacated and the tracks eventually removed to leave the depot buildings to be vandalised.

In December 1988 new sidings were laid on the site for the storage of track maintenance units, with the shed structure nearest to the main lines brought back into use. The facilities were still in use in March 1994, when an early morning Paddington to Swansea HST was photographed passing the site. However, the former diesel depot structures were subsequently vacated and finally demolished in 1995. *GPD/DCG*

NEWPORT (DOCK STREET): Newport's street and dock railways were developed in the second half of the 19th century to serve the numerous wharves to be found along the western bank of the River Usk. The initial section was opened by the Monmouthshire Railway, then others by the Pontypridd, Caerphilly & Newport Railway, later to become the Alexandra (Newport & South Wales) Dock & Railway Company. A passenger station at Dock Street was opened in May 1855 but was closed by March 1880, when the Sirhowy Valley trains were re-routed into the rebuilt Newport High Street station. The goods facilities survived until closure in November 1966. On Saturday 8 May 1971 the RCTS employed a Swindon three-car Cross Country DMU (Class 120) for its Eastern Valleys Rail Tour and the unit is pictured during a photo stop near Dock Street. The sidings at Loco Yard Junction are visible in the background and the line to the Western Valleys curves round to the right.

Octopus Bridge had provided the vantage point for the 1971 photograph, but the bridge had been demolished and the site cleared for the construction of a road traffic island by the spring of 1994. *Hugh Ballantyne/DCG*

NEWPORT PILL MPD: Originally built and opened in 1898 by the Alexandra Docks Railway, Newport Pill shed was located at the north end of the docks it served. At nationalisation its allocation comprised over 50 locomotives, the majority being 0-6-0 Pannier tanks. A depot visit on 21 August 1955 provided this view of the shed area with Nos 6732, 1506, 6731, 5733 and 5706 visible. The GWR-pattern coaling stage added in 1929 can be seen on the right to the rear of the line of locomotives.

Closure came on 17 June 1963 and the buildings were later demolished and the site cleared to accommodate a road transport depot. Electricity pylons and the famous transporter bridge still dominate the skyline. *W. Potter/GPD*

Left MARSHFIELD was the only intermediate station between Newport and Cardiff, having opened in 1917 and providing platforms on the main lines only. On 8 July 1951 ex-GWR 'Hall' Class No 5953 *Dunley Hall* speeds through with a Cardiff-bound passenger working.

The station was closed to passengers from 10 August 1959 and the goods yard situated on the up side of the station site was in turn closed to general freight traffic in January 1965. On 21 April 1995 Rail Express Systems (Res) Class 47/7 No 47779 passes the location with the 1353 Plymouth to Crewe via Cardiff Mail service. *R. O. Tuck/DCG*

Our final illustration of this volume shows that the former station site at Marshfield was cleared even before the end of the steam era. It was also, rather appropriately, the last photograph of a steam-hauled scheduled freight working taken by our contributor, prior to the total switch to diesel traction in South Wales. On 28 August 1965 ex-LMS Stanier '8F' 2-8-0 No 48702 catches the late evening sun and provides a splendid sight of a steam-hauled freight on the main line as it heads west towards Glamorganshire. *R. O. Tuck*

Also by Don Gatehouse and Geoff Dowling

British Railways Past and Present No 28
Mid and South Glamorgan

Available from December 1995

INDEX OF LOCATIONS